The Gender Gap

ISSUES

Volume 154

Series Editor

Lisa Firth

Independence

Educational Publishers
Cambridge

First published by Independence
The Studio, High Green
Great Shelford
Cambridge CB22 5EG
England

© Independence 2008

British Library Cataloguing in Publication Data
The Gender Gap – (Issues Series)
I. Firth, Lisa II. Series
305.3

ISBN 978 1 86168 441 7

Printed in Great Britain
MWL Print Group Ltd

Cover
The illustration on the front cover is by
Don Hatcher.

CONTENTS

Useful information for readers

Dear Reader,

Issues: The Gender Gap

Gender equality has come a long way since the 1970s: however, inequalities do still exist. Although girls outperform boys in education, this does not translate into a career advantage, with women being paid on average 17% less than men. In addition, statistics show that women are still more likely than men to take responsibility for housework and childcare. This book examines equality issues at home, at work, at school and in law.

The purpose of Issues

The Gender Gap is the one hundred and fifty-fourth volume in the **Issues** series. The aim of this series is to offer up-to-date information about important issues in our world. Whether you are a regular reader or new to the series, we do hope you find this book a useful overview of the many and complex issues involved in the topic.

Titles in the **Issues** series are resource books designed to be of especial use to those undertaking project work or requiring an overview of facts, opinions and information on a particular subject, particularly as a prelude to undertaking their own research.

The information in this book is not from a single author, publication or organisation; the value of this unique series lies in the fact that it presents information from a wide variety of sources, including:

⇨ Government reports and statistics
⇨ Newspaper articles and features
⇨ Information from think-tanks and policy institutes
⇨ Magazine features and surveys
⇨ Website material
⇨ Literature from lobby groups and charitable organisations.*

Critical evaluation

Because the information reprinted here is from a number of different sources, readers should bear in mind the origin of the text and whether the source is likely to have a particular bias or agenda when presenting information (just as they would if undertaking their own research). It is hoped that, as you read about the many aspects of the issues explored in this book, you will critically evaluate the information presented. It is important that you decide whether you are being presented with facts or opinions. Does the writer give a biased or an unbiased report? If an opinion is being expressed, do you agree with the writer?

The Gender Gap offers a useful starting point for those who need convenient access to information about the many issues involved. However, it is only a starting point. Following each article is a URL to the relevant organisation's website, which you may wish to visit for further information.

Kind regards,

Lisa Firth
Editor, **Issues** series

*Please note that Independence Publishers has no political affiliations or opinions on the topics covered in the **Issues** series, and any views quoted in this book are not necessarily those of the publisher or its staff.*

Upbringing versus biology

Do gender-specific behaviours arise in children because of biological factors or because infants are encouraged (consciously or subconsciously) to conform to particular gender roles? Information from the Wellcome Trust

By about 18 months, most children begin to display gender-specific behaviours. Boys will tend to choose vehicles or construction toys to play with; girls go for dolls. These behaviours appear so early that some suggest that they must be innate, while others argue that they simply reflect parental influences or the child's desire to conform.

These possible causes are difficult to study. With human subjects, controlled studies cannot be carried out to compare the impact of, say, prenatal hormones or particular styles of parenting.

By about 18 months, most children begin to display gender-specific behaviours

---

Observational studies suggest that parents tend to treat male and female children differently from birth, even without realising it.

On the other hand, girls with congenital adrenal hyperplasia – who have relatively high testosterone levels – are typically more 'tomboyish' than other girls. Early in life, they also show greater preference for 'male' toys, even when parents encourage them to play with gender-appropriate toys. Such studies argue in favour of a biological effect mediated through hormones.

Studies on animals support this idea. For example, rats show sex-specific behaviours, but these disappear if the effect of sex hormones before birth is blocked. Some primates have recently been shown to demonstrate sex-specific choices - boy monkeys preferring trucks and girl monkeys preferring dolls. Although primates may have social structures, this is more likely to reflect innate preferences.

One way to tease apart cultural/environmental and genetic/biological influences is through twin studies. By comparing characteristics in identical twins (which share all their genes) and non-identical twins (which share half their genes), researchers can estimate the relative contributions of genes and environment (though such studies do not say anything about what these influences actually are).

A recent study of 4000 pre-school children confirmed that sex-typed behaviours were influenced by both environmental and genetic factors (the latter affecting girls particularly strongly). It seems likely that the genetic effects are mediated through the action of hormones in the developing baby.

⇨ Information from the Wellcome Trust. Visit www.wellcome.ac.uk for more information.

© *Wellcome Trust*

The gender gap

Although often used interchangeably, 'sex' and 'gender' have different meanings

Sex is a biological concept based on, for example, the possession of particular types of sex cells and organs. Usually (but not always) two sexes can be identified in animals: males and females. In some hermaphrodite species, individuals produce both eggs and sperm.

Gender is based on traits or characteristics that may be either masculine (strength, courage) or feminine (nurturing, caring), and encompasses both what people imagine themselves to be and the social context in which they find themselves.

Gender traits show considerable variation, and each person will be a combination of masculine and feminine traits of varying degrees.

There is a tendency to see masculinity as the definition or 'ideal state' of maleness but that may be unhelpful. If males show more masculine characteristics (and females more feminine qualities), this could reflect biological sex differences or the impact of factors such as upbringing or pressures to conform to 'expected' gender roles.

There is usually little conflict between sex and gender, but this is not always so. Some people may passionately believe that the sex they feel they are is different from the body that nature has given them. This can lead people to opt for sex change surgery.

Another complexity arises when the normal sex determination processes are disrupted, creating intersex individuals.

⇨ The above information is reprinted with kind permission from the Wellcome Trust. Visit www.wellcome.ac.uk for more information.

© *Wellcome Trust*

The gender agenda

The unfinished revolution

The way we live has transformed dramatically in the last 30 years. The roles of men and women have changed in a fast-paced social revolution but life around us has not caught up. This revolution is unfinished and we are all paying the price.

Individually we face the challenge of fitting together work, children, family and relationships. Collectively, we face the challenges of an ageing population, a 24/7 global economy and concerns about our fragmented communities.

Increasingly 'breadwinner dads' and 'stay at home mums' are a thing of the past. Fathers today want to spend more time with their children but long working hours make this hard. Most mothers want or need to go to work, but despite their qualifications, many have to trade down pay if they want to work part-time. Also many adults, women *and* men, need and want to provide more support to their older relatives. But our workplaces, services and institutions are designed for an age when 'women stayed at home', which makes it a struggle for those trying to combine work and care.

And there is inequality in other areas of our modern life. Men are still paid more than women; every year thousands of pregnant workers are treated unfairly; and thousands of women are sexually harassed at work. Although half of us want to work more flexible hours, many of us still cannot achieve this; public policies, which could do so much to make life fairer, often fail to do so; and economic and political power is still mostly held by men. And we should never forget that gender inequality still underpins life and death issues – every month seven women are killed by their partner, ex-partner or lover.

Tackling this would make sense for our social health and financial wealth, as well as bringing justice. Whilst our own lives are made more difficult by these inequalities, Britain will also lose out economically if we don't tackle them. A country that doesn't use its full potential, that channels women into low-paid work, forces families to struggle to cope, and loses the skills of those who cannot work and care, will fall behind.

We need to transform our workplaces, our services and our communities. Without this we all face the consequences of the unfinished revolution.

Increasingly 'breadwinner dads' and 'stay at home mums' are a thing of the past

---

The good news is that we can change things for the future. If we achieve the following goals for women and men in the next 10 years we can complete the revolution:

⇨ close the income gap between men and women;

⇨ give better support to modern families;

⇨ modernise public services so they meet women's and men's needs;

⇨ provide equal access to justice and safety;

⇨ share power equally between men and women.

In addition, transgender people face inequalities that are not totally captured in the goals above, so we also have a specific goal to improve transgender equality within the next 10 years:

⇨ ensure transgender people enjoy equal rights and access to services.

Closing the income gap

Women who work full-time earn, on average, 17% less per hour than men working full-time. For women who work part-time, the gap in pay relative to full-time men is a huge 38% per hour. The causes of the pay gap are complex – in part to do with discrimination; in part because women are more likely than men to work in low-paid sectors; and in part because women often have to 'trade down' or face other work and pay penalties once they become mothers. The average woman working full-time could lose out on £330,000 over the course of her working life. These aren't figures from the 1970s before equal pay laws came into force – they're current and show the shocking income gap that persists between men and women. The problem affects us throughout our lives because lower pay means that women face a pensions gap too – their retirement income is 40% less than men's. And some groups of women face an even bigger income gap – for example, Pakistani women are paid less on average for full-time work than white British women and substantially less than white British men.

Until we close these glaring income gaps and fundamentally change Britain's workplaces, our choices will remain limited. Men and women will not be able to organise family life in a way that works for them, older women will continue to be less independent than men and with the under-use of women's skills our country will become less productive in a tougher global economy.

We need to transform the income gap in the next 10 years so that:

⇨ Full- and part-time gender pay gaps are on course to be eliminated in time to benefit the current generation of working women;

⇨ Having children does not mean economic inequality for women;

⇨ Becoming a carer does not lead to economic inequality;

⇨ Flexible working is available in all types of work, including senior roles;

⇨ Women are found in as wide a range of jobs as men and no jobs are overwhelmingly done just by women or just by men;

⇨ Pregnancy discrimination, sexual harassment and other forms of workplace discrimination are on course to be eliminated;

⇨ The pay, participation and promotion gaps between ethnic minority and white women have closed;

⇨ The gender pension gap is on course to be eliminated by a reformed pension system;

⇨ Employers routinely check the equality of their workplaces and take action on the results;

⇨ Where discrimination occurs, people know their rights and have effective access to justice.

Supporting modern families

30 years ago families were typically made up of a mum, dad and their children. Modern families today are more diverse, with many more single parents, stepfamilies and same-sex parents. Roles within the family are changing too, with most new dads no longer seeing their role just as breadwinner and wanting to share caring. We are also living longer and are likely to need more support as we age – as well as wanting to help out with the care of our own parents, relatives and friends.

More than 8 out of 10 of us believe it's hard for parents and carers to balance work and family life. We also think caring remains undervalued and still mainly falls to women. And most people believe that working and caring will be even harder in 10 years. For women especially, sex equality is a thin veneer that cracks when they take on caring responsibilities.

We need to transform the support we give to Britain's diverse families. In 10 years' time we want to see:

⇨ Public policies and workplace practices routinely designed to meet the real needs of mothers, fathers and carers in families of all types;

⇨ Parents and carers from all backgrounds feeling better supported and having real choices about how to combine work and caring roles;

⇨ Men able to take equally active caring roles as women and doing so in practice by, for example, using transferable maternity leave;

⇨ A greater sharing of caring, domestic work and resources between women and men;

⇨ Older or disabled women and men from all backgrounds getting access to good quality care services, and choices about this, including independent living;

⇨ That where discrimination occurs, people know their rights and have effective access to justice.

Modernising public services

Our public services don't always meet the different needs of women and men in the modern world. Public services are part of the infrastructure that supports our lives. Not being able to access services can have knock-on effects that prevent us fulfilling our potential. Public transport is still geared up to supporting men's lives more then women's; childcare places are scarce; men are reluctant to visit their GP; and young people are channelled into traditional 'male' and 'female' jobs from school. Public policies and services are not meeting the challenges of changing lives. They were never designed with the different needs of men and women in mind. That needs to change.

The introduction of the Gender Equality Duty means that public bodies will have to take account of the different needs of men and women when they design and deliver services. But there is more that can be done to make public services fit for the 21st century.

In the next 10 years we want to see:

⇨ A welfare system that supports modern families in all their diversity by making sure there is, for example: enough good quality, affordable childcare; sufficient paid leave for both mothers and fathers; and a social care system that supports independent living;

⇨ Public services that are free of gender stereotypes so women, men, girls and boys can fulfil their potential;

⇨ An 'education gap' between girls and boys that has closed, with boys' attainment, including that of ethnic minority boys, matching that of girls;

⇨ Health services that are equally accessible to men and women, to improve health outcomes for both sexes;

⇨ Sexual health and contraception services provided appropriately to both men and women, with safe access to abortion services for women when needed;

⇨ A transport system planned around women's needs as well as men's;

⇨ That only organisations with good equality records win public sector contracts, to ensure equality in public services regardless of who delivers the service;

⇨ That where discrimination and inequality occur, the gender equality duty is effectively tackling it, people know their rights and have effective access to justice.

Tackling violence and ensuring safe communities

Our communities should be safe for us all. This means safe streets, safe homes, safe schools, safe facilities and

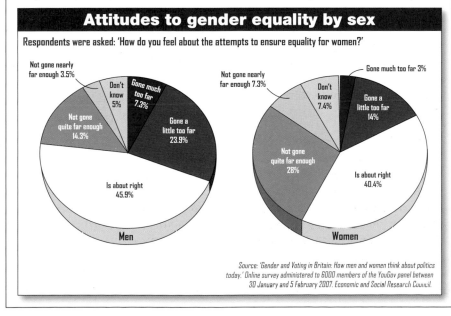

Attitudes to gender equality by sex

Respondents were asked: 'How do you feel about the attempts to ensure equality for women?'

Men:
- Not gone nearly far enough 3.5%
- Don't know 5%
- Gone much too far 7.3%
- Not gone quite far enough 14.3%
- Gone a little too far 23.9%
- Is about right 45.9%

Women:
- Not gone nearly far enough 7.3%
- Don't know 7.4%
- Gone much too far 3%
- Gone a little too far 14%
- Not gone quite far enough 28%
- Is about right 40.4%

Source: 'Gender and Voting in Britain: How men and women think about politics today.' Online survey administered to 6000 members of the YouGov panel between 30 January and 5 February 2007. Economic and Social Research Council.

safe workplaces. We must eradicate domestic violence as a priority, police it seriously and prosecute it properly. People should have enough confidence in the criminal justice system to come forward to report rape or sexual assault, knowing their attackers will face justice. No one should be forced into marriage or be trafficked into forced prostitution.

At the same time our justice system must treat women and men fairly. Women should not be imprisoned for lesser crimes than men, and when parents have to go to prison, they should be able to stay in touch with their children.

We must do more to help young people, especially young men, to stay out of crime. Resources should be allocated to preventing sexual violence and promoting zero tolerance of it, for example in schools, prisons and through the media.

Our institutions, families, schools and public services must challenge the kinds of attitudes that promote or condone violence against women and girls.

In 10 years' time we want to see:
⇨ That gender-based violence is no longer considered acceptable;
⇨ The criminal justice system tackling gender-based crimes effectively, including: a significant reduction in the incidence of domestic violence; an increase in the proportion of reported rapes that are successfully prosecuted; and more action to prevent trafficking of women and girls for forced prostitution;
⇨ That forced marriage is rare and survivors are better supported;
⇨ That gender-based violence is recognised as grounds for asylum;
⇨ Women and men being treated fairly and appropriately by the criminal justice system in sentencing and prison arrangements;
⇨ That offending rates of young men have reduced;
⇨ That women's fear of crime is no longer limiting their day-to-day activities outside the home;
⇨ That schools are successfully challenging attitudes that lead to sexual bullying and gender-based violence.

Sharing power

There is a power gap in our institutions and workplaces. Women are much less likely than men to reach the top of their professions. Only 10% of directorships of FTSE 100 companies are held by women. In today's workplace requesting flexible working can still spell career death for many women. Instead they often have to 'trade down' when they take on caring roles and then lose out on the top jobs. When it comes to political representation the situation is no better. Currently less than 20% of MPs are female, and at the current rate of change it will take up to 200 years to achieve an equal number of men and women in the Westminster Parliament. For certain groups of women, for example ethnic minority women, their representation is even lower.

The power gap needs to be closed, with true representation for all groups of women, including ethnic minority women, disabled women, lesbians, and women of all ages and faiths. Shared power would be an important sign of gender equality – it will show us that we have managed to complete the social revolution.

In 10 years' time we want to see:
⇨ The 'gender power gap' in political representation to be on track to close within a generation;
⇨ The 'power gap' between women and men in top jobs to be closing and on course to be eliminated;
⇨ Representation to increase for women from all social and ethnic groups as the gender power gap closes;
⇨ Flexible ways of working to have become 'the norm' in all sectors and levels of seniority;
⇨ Women and men to have an equal voice in their communities;
⇨ Voluntary organisations to give sex equality a high priority and a strong voice.

Eliminating discrimination against transgender people

Transgender people face the same gender problems as other women and men but often face huge additional prejudice on a daily basis.

To tackle these concerns, we want the Commission for Equality and Human Rights to make sure that in 10 years' time:
⇨ Discrimination, harassment and stereotyping of transgender people has reduced significantly and is on course to be eliminated;
⇨ Transgender people have equal protection under the law to other men and women and the legal definitions cover everyone who identifies as transgender;
⇨ Public policies and services, including health and education, are meeting the needs of transgender people;
⇨ Transgender people enjoy the same level of respect as other men and women, and employers and service providers have a good understanding of their concerns.

We must complete the unfinished revolution

Action is needed now. Our systems and institutions must catch up with the way we live so that all women and men can achieve equality. The Equal Opportunities Commission is calling on the Government, the business community, service providers and the Commission for Equality and Human Rights to continue taking the necessary steps to enable gender equality to be achieved:
⇨ close the income gap between men and women;
⇨ give better support to modern families;
⇨ modernise public services so they meet women's and men's needs;
⇨ provide equal access to justice and safety;
⇨ share power equally between men and women;
⇨ ensure transgender people enjoy equal rights and access to services.

That's the Gender Agenda. It's time to complete the unfinished revolution. *July 2007*

⇨ The above information is reprinted with kind permission from the Equal Opportunities Commission, now part of the Commission for Equality and Human Rights. Visit www.equalityhumanrights.com for more information.

© Equal Opportunities Commission

Equality for girls?

YWCA welcomes the new Gender Equality Duty

The Gender Equality Duty (GED) comes into force on 6 April 2007. It means all public bodies, including hospitals, local authorities, schools and the police must take gender into consideration when providing services. YWCA England & Wales welcomes this new duty, but is concerned that it will not address the specific needs of disadvantaged young girls.

Lucy Russell, YWCA's policy development officer, comments: 'The approach to gender equality cannot be the same for all women. The needs of a white, middle-class, 50-year-old woman are very different to a 15-year-old Pakistani girl. We particularly call on public authorities to support single-sex work, as it is often the most effective way of meeting teenage girls' needs.'

Single-sex work is particularly good for confidence building, challenging gender stereotypes, and tackling sensitive issues like sexual health or abuse, when mixed gender groups may not be appropriate. Work that best meets the needs of a certain group, including single-sex work, is still legal and meets the gender equality duty guidelines. For the duty to be implemented in a meaningful way the provision of specific, targeted services is essential.

Case study

Hazel Gibbs from West Kent featured in a recent piece in the *Guardian* about the Gender Equality Duty.

Hazel, now 22, was expelled from two schools and left with no qualifications and little careers advice. It was only by attending YWCA in West Kent that she gained qualifications and received the information and support that she needed to eventually go to college. She originally looked at hairdressing as an option, but realised that this wasn't for her as she had always been interested in DIY but hadn't known how to get into it, 'or even that I could make a career out of it'. With support from YWCA staff Hazel is now on a painting and decorating course at her local college and doing really well. She is at last realising her potential, aiming for a secure future and challenging gender stereotyping.

5 April 2007

➪ Information from the YWCA. Visit www.ywca.org.uk for more information.

© YWCA

Changes since the 1970s

Then	Now
Only one in four of both boys and girls in England and Wales passed five O levels by the time they left school.	49% of boys and 59% of girls in the UK gain five high grade GCSEs or equivalent by age 16.
Nine out of ten men and six out of ten women of working age were in employment.	Employment rates are 79% for men and 70% for women of working age.
Around one in ten professionals were women.	Women hold two-fifths of professional jobs.
The gap between women's and men's full-time hourly pay was 29%.	Women earn on average 17% per hour less than men for full-time work.
Two-thirds of workers in public administration were men and 55% of workers in the distribution sector were women.	The workforce in wholesale and retail is almost equally split between women and men, as is that in public administration and defence.
Half of mothers with dependent children worked, including over a quarter of mothers of under-fives.	Two-thirds of mothers with dependent children work and 55% of those with children under five.
There were only 27 women MPs or 4.3% of the UK Parliament.	Women's representation in the UK Parliament has reached one in five.

Source: *Facts about Women and Men in Great Britain 2006 (EOC).*

Prevalence of sex discrimination

Sex discrimination rife and equality will take generations, says axed commission

Sex equality will take generations to achieve at the current 'painfully slow' rate of progress, the Equal Opportunities Commission (EOC) said today in a final report before being wound up by the government after more than 30 years fighting gender bias across British society.

It found discrimination is still rife in politics, employment and public services, and stark gender gaps exist at work and at home. After analysing 22 measurements of the nation's progress towards sex equality, the commission found:

⇨ A 'power gap' in parliament, where only 20% of MPs are women. At the current rate, it will take 195 years for this to close and 65 years to achieve a gender balance in the boardrooms of the top companies listed in the FTSE 100 index;

Discrimination is still rife in politics, employment and public services, and stark gender gaps exist at work and at home

⇨ A 'pensions gap' that leaves retired women with 40% less income than male contemporaries; this gap could take 45 years to close;

⇨ A 'part-time pay gap' will take 25 years to close and the 'full-time pay gap' 20 years, in a system that now pays women 38% less per hour than men for working part time and 17% for full-timers;

⇨ A 'health gap', disadvantaging men, that may never close unless the NHS adopts more male-friendly practices to address the problem that men aged 16-44 are less than half as likely as women to

By John Carvel, Social Affairs Editor

consult their GP, resulting in later diagnosis of serious illnesses.

The EOC is due to be absorbed in October into the Commission for Equality and Human Rights, an all-purpose, anti-discrimination body chaired by Trevor Phillips, former chairman of the Commission for Racial Equality. Campaigners fear gender equality may be downplayed by the new body, which will also be responsible for combating discrimination on grounds of race, disability and age.

The EOC commissioned the research on the gender gap to influence the new body's priorities. 'This is our big push for them to take note. We will be keeping a close eye on their response,' a spokesman said.

The report said: 'The way we live our lives has transformed dramatically in the last 30 years. New parents expect to share the upbringing of their children and both women and men want to work more flexibly and provide more support for older relatives.

'But life around us has not caught up and we are living with the consequences of an unfinished social revolution. We are still faced with many workplaces, institutions and services designed for an age when women stayed at home. In other areas of modern life, inequality underpins life and death issues. For example, every month seven women are killed by their partner or ex-partner.'

Women are five times more likely to feel unsafe when walking alone in their area after dark. But not all issues of public safety result in advantages for men. Over the past year 13% of young men were victims of violent crime, compared with 7% of young women.

The commission said 45% of pregnant women experience 'tangible discrimination'. Mothers spend 12% more time than fathers looking after children and the 'chores gap' is worsening, with women spending an average 180 minutes a day on housework, against 101 minutes for men.

The EOC set five priorities. They were: closing the income gap between men and women; giving better support to families; modernising public services; providing equal access to justice and safety; and sharing power equally.

Jenny Watson, the commission's chairwoman, said: 'Today, most women work, many men no longer define themselves as breadwinners and both sexes often struggle to find the time they need to care for others in their lives. Despite many advances, Britain's institutions have not caught up with these changes.

'A country that channels women into low-paid work, fails to adequately support families and forces people who want to work flexibly to trade down in jobs pays a high price in terms of child poverty, family breakdown and low productivity. This is a challenge that Gordon Brown's new government urgently needs to address.'

Brendan Barber, general secretary of the TUC, said: 'With men still dominating senior positions in business, politics, and almost every walk of life, it's crucial that achieving gender equality is a top priority for the new commission.'

Harriet Harman, Labour's deputy leader and minister for women, said: 'There is still inequality between men and women in our economy and society that needs to be tackled ... We aim to achieve this by giving women more choices in the workplace, in public life and in the home.'

24 July 2007

Why men should care about gender stereotypes

Alex Gibson considers the harm done by stereotypes of men as beer-swilling, emotionally-stunted brutes

These days you can find things on the internet that you would never see published in a magazine or on television. The cloak of anonymity and the chain-mail culture seems to encourage – among other things – the spread of sexist 'jokes' and stereotypes. The internet abounds with articles taking an apparently humorous look at the kind of things that men and women 'always do'. One particular list that caught my attention was 'Courses For Men, Taught By Women' which included such gems as 'Spelling: Even You Can Get It Right', 'The Weekend And Sports Are Not Synonymous' and 'Parenting Doesn't End With Conception'. Of course there was a parallel list for women, but it was the list about men that got me thinking.

Let's not kid ourselves here: men as well as women are limited by gender stereotypes. The idea of men as stupid and sex-obsessed is an enduring generalisation that is allowed to flourish in – dare I say it – a much more brazen way than the stereotypes about women, mainly because no man ever stands up and says: 'Hey, that's sexist and it offends me!' The problem is, while women are encouraged to reject the ludicrous ideas that are held about them, men are supposed to embrace them.

In the creation of gender stereotypes, men really missed a trick. Male-dominated culture has cultivated an image of women that I'm sure you're familiar with: endlessly shopping, outspoken (which for women essentially amounts to expressing a strong opinion about anything), money-draining, demanding and contrary. The classic picture that we are presented with in television, films, advertisements and practically every other medium for disseminating information, is of women as a burden,

the irritating nagging voice in the back of your head that won't leave you alone even for a second and scolds you for leaving the toilet seat up.

But Christ, guys, have you seen what we're supposed to be like? Looking solely at stereotypes, men do not fare well. I would never dare to suggest that men have a harder time than women in general society, because that's just patently untrue, but in terms of stereotypes we fail utterly. Male perceptions of women are designed to make us feel smug in our superiority, but the way we've chosen to label ourselves should make any man feel thoroughly humiliated and ashamed of his gender.

Men are often characterised as spoiled, helpless brats utterly unable to perform simple household tasks, too stupid to remember anniversaries and appointments and completely unable to understand these strange female creatures and their hysterical emotions. We're base brutes ruled by our overactive sex drives who simply can't help being crass and immature, because that is the way God made us. Basically, we are mentally deficient lumps who require a female carer to function in society. This is precisely the kind of ridiculous stereotype that,

if applied to women, would be torn to shreds in intelligent debate. So why don't men object at being labelled emotional morons totally in thrall to their basest instincts?

Men as well as women are limited by gender stereotypes

Here's the thing: men don't have anything remotely equivalent to feminism. From an early age, women are aware of their gender and what it means for their lives, far more than men are. Feminism encourages women to shed gender stereotypes and consider themselves as individuals. Men simply don't think about gender. Why would you, when it rarely impacts in a noticeable way on your life? Very rarely is your progress barred because you are a man and it is true that male culture generally does not promote frank and open discussion of such issues.

Many men aren't feminists simply because it has never occurred to them that they should be: when you're not faced every day with the challenges thrown up by gender inequality it is very easy to think: 'Well, we've changed the law so we have equality now.' I know it sounds ridiculous – you'd never hear anyone claiming that racism died when it became illegal to racially discriminate, for example, but it is a pretty common thought. If women are under-represented in highly paid jobs, it is because these changes take time to filter through, or because there were no female candidates qualified enough to take the positions, not because sexism is still endemic. I'm ashamed to say that I used to think like that: sexism isn't a major issue for men and it is easy to brush it off in this manner.

So men don't get to discuss gender in the same way that women do, and there's a reason for this. Male culture – the kind promoted by *FHM*, *Nuts*, tabloid newspapers and the like – abhors debate on anything remotely intelligent. Men are hemmed in on two fronts: by the stereotypes the media pin on them and the pervading culture they have created for themselves that leads to such stereotypes in the first place.

The 'real man' is encouraged to reject intelligence and self-improvement as ideas firmly in the domain of women, creating a wonderful self-perpetuating cycle of idiocy. Creativity, interest in academia and a desire to learn are all frowned upon by a male culture where footballers are considered legitimate role models. Reading? Boring. Poetry? Something for 'gays' and 'nerds', lesser men in the eyes of their peers. Lesbianism? A spectator sport designed for the titillation of men. For a man to become all that is good and masculine, he must revel in his own stupidity and inability to function as an acceptable human being. The ultimate goal of a 'real man' is to spend his life slumped in front of the television, beer in hand, watching the football and waiting for his wife to cook him something appropriately manly. I always found it amusing that massive slabs of meat are considered more fitting for a man's meal than those no-good effeminate vegetables, but it's the only part of this rotten aspirational model that makes me smile. We're meant to feel good about this? This is the goal of a man's life? No thanks.

I'm by no means the only one who rejects the idea of a 'real man' embodying all these things, but – and here's the crucial point – despite the fact that there are many of us who grew up resenting the dominance of this (to borrow a phrase) idiocracy, we are content to let it continue. The people labelled nerds or geeks for not wanting the worthless life that traditional masculinity offers them, allow themselves to be ostracised for it. Yes, it is gratifying to look back at those people who, during your teenage years, were the epitome of the classic

ideas of manhood. They mostly now live dead-end lives, but don't forget that their culture is still the dominant one among men. Intelligent men who don't subscribe to this ideal of a 'real man' as a rugged emotionally-stunted womaniser probably outnumber those who do, and yet it's still not quite alright for a man to be interested in poetry, be a feminist, or know how to darn socks (hey, I'm a student, it's all about saving money!). A lot of men don't realise that instead of feeling troubled because they fail to fit this mould, they should be rejoicing in breaking free of it.

Feminism has taught women who are prepared to listen that their traditional gender roles needn't be upheld as a good thing, that to branch out from the way women are 'supposed to be' is a way of marking yourself out as independent and intelligent. Men simply haven't got anything to raise their consciousness about this issue: we are still, as a gender, wedded to these damaging ideas of manhood that do nothing but churn out generation after generation of men unable to aspire to any goals worth having.

So what can we, a group of individuals who clearly care about gender equality and despise gender stereotypes, do about this? Granted, it isn't fair of men to expect feminism to deal with male gender stereotypes as well as female ones, and I don't for a second think they should, but it is a problem that affects all of us. A prevailing culture of stupidity just isn't good enough for men or women, even if the former often don't realise it. Men can be the attentive and understanding partners that women want, and it is a tragic shame that

society has conditioned the male mind to reject this sensitivity as weak and inappropriate. The change that needs to be made is cultural, but that doesn't make it any less difficult. Let's stop putting sports stars on a pedestal and start celebrating poets, writers, scientists and artists. Let's start converting some more men to feminism: considering the problems caused by gender for women is a fantastic way to make them think about how gender also holds them back. It worked for me.

It is easier to see the problem than come up with a solution, but just letting male culture continue down this road isn't good enough for me. Guys, unless we learn to throw out these damaging ideas of manhood and learn to aspire to something better, when we truly have equality of the sexes we're going to look very shabby and stupid compared to women. I'm used to being ashamed and disappointed by the way my gender acts – I don't want to add embarrassment to that list.

About the author

Alex Gibson is a modern history student at Magdalen College, Oxford. He is very proud to add feminism to a list of 'isms' he cares passionately about, and is quite fond of making his friends uncomfortable in the pub by talking about it
2 February 2008

⇨ The above information is reprinted with kind permission from Alex Gibson and The F Word, featuring articles on contemporary feminism. Visit www.thefword.org.uk for more.
© Alex Gibson

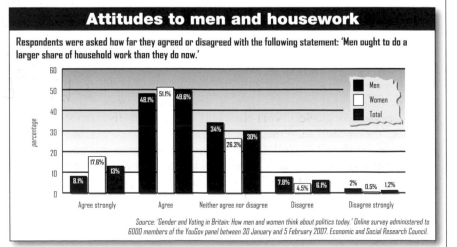

Attitudes to men and housework

Respondents were asked how far they agreed or disagreed with the following statement: 'Men ought to do a larger share of household work than they do now.'

Source: 'Gender and Voting in Britain: How men and women think about politics today.' Online survey administered to 6000 members of the YouGov panel between 30 January and 5 February 2007. Economic and Social Research Council.

Do men speak Martian?

Kenan Malik reviews *The Myth of Mars and Venus: Do Men And Women Really Speak Different Languages?* by Deborah Cameron

My four-year-old daughter, like many girls of her age, has become obsessed by all things pink. Why? It's in her genes, says the neuroscientist Anya Hurlbert. In August, virtually every newspaper splashed Hurlbert's latest research that showed, would you believe it, that women like pink and men prefer blue.

Back in our hunter-gatherer days, Hurlbert speculated, 'women were the primary gatherers and would have benefited from an ability to home in on ripe, red fruits'. Stone Age men, on the other hand, 'would have a natural preference for a clear blue sky because it signalled good weather'.

There is only one problem with this argument. A hundred years ago boys liked pink while girls preferred blue. As the *Ladies Home Journal* put it in 1918, 'pink being a more decided and stronger colour is more suitable for the boy, while blue, which is more delicate and dainty, is prettier for the girl'.

It is not difficult to mock the argument that men and women wear pink and blue genes. Yet this is only the more absurd form of claims about gender differences that most people accept as self-evident.

We all know, for instance, that women are better communicators than men. They talk more. They talk about people and relationships, where men tend to talk only about facts and things. And they try to be inclusive and cooperative rather than competitive and assertive.

Think again, says Deborah Cameron, professor of language and communication at the University of Oxford.

Her new book unpicks what she calls *The Myth of Mars and Venus*. The myth began as the whimsical title of a best-selling self-help book – John Gray's *Men are from Mars, Women are from Venus*. Fifteen years on, the metaphor has mutated to scientific fact. Psychologists now routinely talk of the 'male brain' and the 'female brain' and about men and women being akin to different species.

Such stark distinctions, however, are belied by the facts.

There are clearly anatomical differences between the brains of men and women, differences that have evolutionary roots. Yet, careful analysis of all the research on how the genders approach tasks such as vocabulary, verbal reasoning and assertiveness of speech reveal mostly small or non-existent differences.

Children do not come neatly packaged in black and white, pink and blue, Mars and Venus. Nor does the world

---

It also shows that the best predictor of the kind of language someone might use is not their sex but their social role. Where men are in jobs that involve facilitating others – such as teaching or broadcasting – they use stereotypically 'female' forms of speech.

Where women find themselves in positions of authority – as in politics or business – they are assertive and competitive, contrary to the popular myth that women bring a uniquely feminine touch to management and public debate.

The crucial distinction, Cameron suggests, is not so much that between men and women as that between the public and private realms. The public sphere often requires assertive, competitive language and because this sphere has historically been the province of men, so such language has been associated with maleness.

In the private arena, relationships, emotions and feelings become more important. And these are seen as female linguistic attributes because of the association of women and domesticity.

Could it not be that men dominate the public sphere because they are naturally assertive and women the private because they are better at handling intimacy? Unlikely, suggests Cameron, as the same individual can switch between different kinds of talk depending on what is required of him or her.

The debate, Cameron insists, is not one between nature and nurture. While evolutionary psychologists see the roots of gender differences in evolutionary history, others, especially self-help gurus, see the distinction as cultural. 'The biological determinist and the cultural relativist', Cameron writes, 'may travel by different routes, but they arrive at the same destination.'

A key problem is that 'We actively look for differences, and seek out sources which discuss them' but 'are much less attentive to, and less interested in hearing about, similarities between men and women.' This inevitably biases both research and the interpretations of data.

As for my daughter, she is obsessed not just with all things pink, but also with dinosaurs, racing cars and space travel. When she grows up she wants to be an astronaut with a pink rocket.

Children do not come neatly packaged in black and white, pink and blue, Mars and Venus. Nor does the world.

8 November 2007

© *Telegraph Group Limited, London 2008*

Today's girls prefer to look sexy rather than be clever

This generation is being sexualised before they reach their teens, a trend which threatens their self-worth, warns a top US female academic

By Amelia Hill, Social Affairs Correspondent

Women have fought for decades to be treated as men's equals. Yet today's girls are being told that female empowerment simply comes from being 'sexy', according to a new book by the managing editor of the *Harvard Law Review*.

In *Prude: How The Sex-Obsessed Culture Damages Girls*, Carol Platt Liebau says popular culture is undermining girls' sense of worth in their most vulnerable, formative years and glorifying destructive behaviour.

'The overwhelming lesson teenagers are now learning from the world around them is that being "sexy" is the ultimate accolade, trumping intelligence, character and all other accomplishments at every stage of a woman's life,' said Liebau, a political analyst and the review's first female managing editor. 'The new female imperative is that it is only through promiscuity and sexual aggression that girls can achieve admiration and recognition.' She cites films such as *Cruel Intentions* and *Mean Girls*, the music and videos of Britney Spears, Christina Aguilera and Lil' Kim, and advertisements such as the dominatrix-themed campaign for the teenage fashion house bebe, featuring Mischa Barton. 'In a culture that celebrates Paris Hilton, thong underwear and songs like "My Humps" – where the female singer expounds the sexual magnetism of her breasts and buttocks – there's scant recognition or respect for female modesty or achievement that isn't coupled with sex appeal,' she adds.

'Girls are being led to believe they're in control when it comes to sexual relationships,' she continues. 'But they're actually living in a profoundly anti-feminist landscape where girls compete for attention on the basis of how much they are sexually willing to do for the boys.' Liebau's book has won support from feminists, including Ariel Levy, whose book *Female Chauvinist Pigs* denounced what Levy termed a 'raunch culture' that, she said, compels young women to 'compete to look like slags and sluts'. Although Levy was writing about women older than those concerning Liebau, she agrees that the age at which girls are being influenced by the raunch culture is falling. 'Even young girls are the willing, active and conscious participants in a tawdry, tarty, cartoon-like version of female sexuality,' she says.

> **Women have fought for decades to be treated as men's equals. Yet today's girls are being told that female empowerment simply comes from being 'sexy'**

In *Prude*, to be published in Britain by Centre Street Books this month, Liebau questions how society has created a climate in which being raunchy is believed to make girls look cool and in which being called a 'slut' is considered preferable to being labelled a 'prude'. 'By most measures, young women have never had it better. Given the breathtaking opportunities before them and the magnificent advantages they enjoy, it seems Western society has treated young girls with enormous generosity. And in many ways, it has. But not all the changes have been to the good,' she adds. 'Today girls are forced to navigate a minefield more challenging, difficult and pressure-filled than ever before when it comes to sex. Somehow, as society has been revelling in the ubiquity of sex, the very real psychological, emotional and physical impact on young girls of giving too much, too soon, has been discounted,' she said.

Michele Elliott, director of the children's charity Kidscape, agrees. She has launched a campaign against the toy makers responsible for items including a junior pole-dancing kit, thongs for young girls emblazoned with the phrase 'Eye candy' and stationery sets stamped with the bunny logo of Hugh Hefner's Playboy empire.

In her book, Liebau charts how the same 'creeping sexualising' of young girls is endemic across a mass media which, she says, constitutes the main source of information about sex for 13- to 15-year-olds. 'Over the last few decades, the West has experienced an incremental but aggressive sexualising of its culture,' she says. 'Today there exists a status quo in which almost everything seems focused on what's going on "below the waist".'

Although her book has yet to be published in Britain, Liebau is keen to deflect any accusations of prudishness. 'This is about far more than short-term sexual mores,' she says. 'Living in an overly sexualised culture takes a toll on girls. The emphasis on sexiness, revealing fashions and the overvaluing of physical appeal creates pressure to measure up to bone-slim models or celebrities and leads to unrealistic expectations among young women about how their own bodies should actually look.'

9 December 2007

Man made news?

Gender divide revealed in news and political reporting

Research published today by the Fawcett Society shows how few women are 'making the news'.

Man made news

A survey of national media published today shows how few women make the crucial editorial decisions that determine the headlines in both our newspapers and broadcast media. Only 2 out of 17 (12%) editors of national newspapers are women, while all but one of the 17 deputy editors surveyed are men (1).

The major TV and radio news programmes have been marginally more successful at securing a higher proportion of women as presenters; 15 out of 34 (44%) of regular presenters of the leading news programmes are women (2). Yet, editorial decisions for these programmes are being made almost exclusively by men (only one out of 17 – or 6% – of editors of surveyed national TV and radio news programmes is a woman) (3).

Politics – still a boys' club?

The report also shows how the under-representation of women in Westminster is mirrored by a similarly male-dominated political media. Less than 20% of MPs are women and only 26% of political journalists registered at the House of Commons are women (4). Only 2 out of the 16 political editors of the surveyed national newspapers are women (5).

Commenting on the research, Dr Katherine Rake, Director of the Fawcett Society, said:

'Today's survey shows that the media is missing out on the huge pool of female talent, and Britain's viewers, listeners and readers are also missing out as a result. Women must not only be presenting the news, they must be making the decisions that determine what gets broadcast in the first place. We now need to see positive steps taken to make sure that women can break through the glass ceiling and fulfil their potential at the highest level.'

Commenting on the lack of women in the political media, she added:

'We know that women are more dissatisfied with politics and feel more disengaged from the political agenda. Women need to play an equal role in setting the political agenda, both in parliament itself and within the political media. This research shows just how far there is to go until that is achieved.'

A survey of national media shows how few women make the crucial editorial decisions that determine the headlines in both our newspapers and broadcast media

---

Notes

1 Survey of nine daily national newspapers (*Guardian, Independent, Daily Telegraph, Times, Financial Times, Daily Mirror, Daily Mail, Daily Express, Sun*) and eight Sunday national newspapers (*Observer, Independent on Sunday, Sunday Telegraph, Sunday Times, Sunday Mirror, Sunday Express, Mail on Sunday, News of the World*) during the week of 3 December 2007.

2 Survey of TV and radio news programmes [(*One O'Clock News* (BBC 1), *Six O'Clock News* (BBC 1), *Ten O'Clock News* (BBC 1), *Newsnight* (BBC 2), *ITV Lunchtime News* (ITV1), *6.30pm Evening News* (ITV1), *News at 10.30pm* (ITV1), *Channel 4 News* at 12pm, *Channel 4 News* at 7pm, *Five News* at 11.30am, *Five News* at 5.30pm, *Five News* at 7pm, *Sky News Today*, *Sky News at Seven*, *Sky News at Ten*, *Newsbeat* (BBC Radio 1), *Today* (BBC Radio 4), *The World Tonight* (BBC Radio 4), *The World at One* (BBC Radio 4) and *The World This Weekend* (BBC Radio 4)] carried out in the week of 10 December 2007.

3 Survey of TV and radio news programmes (as [2] above). Details were not available for three programmes.

4 As of 6 December 2007, 104 out of the 395 registered lobby journalists were women.

5 Survey of nine daily national newspapers and eight Sunday national newspapers (as [1] above). One position is vacant.

28 December 2007

⇨ The above information is reprinted with kind permission from the Fawcett Society, the UK's leading campaign for equality between women and men. Visit www.fawcettsociety.org.uk for more information.

© *Fawcett Society*

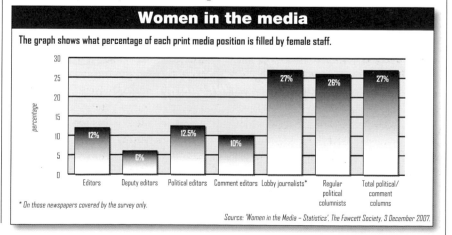

Women in the media

The graph shows what percentage of each print media position is filled by female staff.

Editors 12%, *Deputy editors* 6%, *Political editors* 12.5%, *Comment editors* 10%, *Lobby journalists** 27%, *Regular political columnists* 26%, *Total political/comment columns* 27%

* On those newspapers covered by the survey only.

Source: 'Women in the Media – Statistics', The Fawcett Society, 3 December 2007.

Nearly 50 per cent of all sexual assaults worldwide are against girls under 15. And the rise of religious fundamentalism over the last few years, underpinned sometimes by extreme conservatism when it comes to women's rights, has led not only to the undermining of women's rights, but to increasing numbers of young women murdered by their relatives for supposedly infringing a family code of 'honour'. Young women like Banaz Mahmood, aged 20, who was killed in London in January 2006 by her father, uncle and a family associate because they disapproved of her boyfriend. Her body was found three months later in a suitcase buried in a pit in Birmingham.

Girls' voices

Girls and young women speak out...
'Girl power is about being yourself, sticking up for your rights, and not being afraid of the challenges the world throws at you.'
Girl, 17, Canada

'I don't want to get married and have children, at least not anytime soon... I want to work and study. I don't want to be like another girl I know who is 13 years old and already pregnant.'
Girl, 13, Venezuela

'I never ever understand why boys and girls are not equal to each other. In rural areas elders think that girls are born to give birth and to marry and for cleaning the house. Girls who live in rural areas... are not sent to schools. Their parents are not aware of the changing world yet.'
Girl, 15, Turkey

'The young boy is privileged to have good education, while the girls go to fetch water from streams. One often sees them with big basins of water on their heads to fetch water while the boys play football forgetting that they need water to take a bath. "After all," they say, "why worry when God has blessed us with one or more sisters to relieve us of this task".'
Girl, 16, Cameroon

'My parents used to think that I was their property. They used to abuse me, using words which I cannot repeat without making me cry.'
Girl, 13, Bangladesh

Changes in the law

Over the last 30 years, legislation to protect and prevent discrimination against women and children has been introduced at international and national levels. But few laws refer to girls and young women specifically.

⇨ **1979** The International Convention on the Elimination of all forms of Discrimination Against Women, known as CEDAW, is essentially a bill of women's rights.

⇨ **1989** The United Nations Convention on the Rights of the Child gave under-18s, both boys and girls, protection under the law.

⇨ **1993** The World Conference on Human Rights, in Vienna, stated clearly for the first time that: 'The human rights of women and of the girl-child are an inalienable, integral and indivisible part of universal human rights.'

⇨ **1993** The Declaration on the Elimination of Violence Against Women defined such violence as: 'any act of gender-based violence that results in, or is likely to result in physical, sexual or psychological harm or suffering to women including threats of such acts, coercion or arbitrary deprivation of liberty, whether occurring in public or in private'.

⇨ **1994** The International Conference on Population and Development, Cairo, introduced a 20-year policy agenda that is shaping reproductive and sexual health programmes and policies around the world.

⇨ **1995** The Fourth UN World Conference on Women, Beijing. The Beijing Platform for Action mentions 'rights' approximately 500 times and calls for protection of a wide range of women's rights. It is an important document used by women's groups and governments to work on gender equality.

⇨ **2000** The UN Millennium Declaration committed its signatories to the goal of: 'gender equality and empowerment of women', to universal primary education for both girls and boys and improvements in maternal health, among others. Six out of the eight Millennium Development Goals are in jeopardy if there are not significant improvements in girls' and women's lives by 2015.

Many things have improved as a result of this legislation. Change takes a long time. It is hard to legislate against attitudes or alter the way that girls and young women are viewed at home and in society as a whole.

Missing statistics

While there has been much debate on gender and equality over the last decades, it has obscured two things: first, that although facts and statistics are increasingly collected about women and children, there is very little information out there about girls and young women specifically. As a result, they have been largely ignored as a group, despite the fact that they must constitute at least 25 per cent of the world's population (another statistic that we do not know for certain because figures are not collected).

What we do have are pockets of information from those working in health or education, for example. And it is only when it is collected together that we begin to get a picture of the overall discrimination that girls and young women continue to face; discrimination that can blight or even end their lives.
1 October 2007

⇨ Reprinted by kind permission of the New Internationalist. Copyright New Internationalist. www.newint.org

© New Internationalist

Who does the housework?

Attitudes to gender roles may change but women still do the housework. Information from NatCen

Men have a less traditional view of gender roles than they did 20 years ago. Yet according to the latest British Social Attitudes report, published today by NatCen, women are still far more likely than men to do the household chores. What's more, men tend to say that they do more housework than women think they do.

Men have a less traditional view of gender roles than they did 20 years ago

The report confirms that our behaviour and our views about the roles of men and women are changing. Among couples it is increasingly common for both people to work. Attitudes towards gender roles have changed as well, becoming increasingly liberal among both men and women:

⇨ In 1989, a third of men (32%) agreed with the statement 'a man's job is to earn money; a woman's job is to look after the home and family'. This proportion has nearly halved, standing now at 17%.

⇨ But women continue to have more liberal views about gender roles than men. Four in ten men (41%) and three in ten women (29%) think that 'a pre-school child is likely to suffer if his or her mother works'.

When it comes to doing household chores, our behaviour has changed little:

⇨ Nearly eight in ten people (77%) with partners say that the woman usually or always does the laundry, a similar proportion to that found in 1994 (81%).

⇨ Men and women disagree when it comes to saying how much of the housework they do. Two-thirds of women (68%) say that in their relationship they usually or always do the cleaning – but only 54% of men say this of their partner.

⇨ The most liberal division of labour is found among couples where the woman works full-time, earns more than her partner or has a partner who does not work.

There can be inconsistencies in people's attitudes and their behaviour at home:

⇨ Four in ten women (41%) have liberal views about the role of men and women but a traditional division of labour in their own home. This figure rises to 49% among women who work part-time.

⇨ Not surprisingly, this group are more likely than other women to disagree with their partners over housework: 21% argue about this several times a month or more. This group also find their home life more stressful.

Professor Rosemary Crompton, co-author, comments:

'People's attitudes towards gender roles have clearly changed, but their behaviour lags behind. This is important – a gap between a person's views about gender roles and what actually happens in their own home seems to lead to greater stress at home, for women at least. The women least likely to find their home life stressful are those who have liberal views about gender and who share domestic tasks with their partner.'

This summarises 'Who does the housework? The division of labour within the home' by Rosemary Crompton and Clare Lyonette, in *British Social Attitudes: the 24th Report*, published by Sage for NatCen.
23 January 2008

⇨ The above information is reprinted with kind permission from NatCen, the National Centre for Social Research. Visit www.natcen.ac.uk for more information.
© NatCen

Men's changing lifestyles

Move over competitive mums, now it's the turn of Britain's pushy dads

Pushy parenting used to be the domain of Britain's yummy mummies, but now it is the turn of the dads, as Britain prepares for all-out war at the school gates.

Latest research from Mintel finds that the number one priority for Britain's family man is his kids' exam results – placed well above his own career and health. Exclusive research finds more than half (54%) of men with a young family highlight their kids' exam success as a priority; closely followed by children's out-of-school activities, which are important to just under half (47%) of all family men. Interestingly, Britain's young dads rank their children's achievements well above being successful in their own career (40%) and living a healthy lifestyle (38%).

> **Interestingly, Britain's young dads rank their children's achievements well above being successful in their own career (40%) and living a healthy lifestyle (38%)**

'It seems that many men are putting their children's success well before their own, or at least they would like us to believe as such. Although this interest in kids is encouraging, it could be putting increased pressure on Britain's youngsters. It is also the case that dads want their kids to do better than they themselves did in their own youth,' comments James McCoy, consumer research manager at Mintel.

'Increased competition to get into good schools, especially free ones, could also be a contributing factor,' he adds.

What (wo)men want

It is not just at the school gates where Britain's dads are competing with yummy mummies, as women come under siege in the home as well. Almost a third of men of all ages (30%) say it is important to have their home look the way they want it to, rising to almost four in ten (37%) amongst 30- to 34-year-olds. Not only do Britain's men take pride in their homes, they cook as well. The kitchen is no longer a woman's domain, as no less than 45% of Britain's men say they really enjoy cooking.

What is more, while women have the reputation of being shopaholics, a quarter of all men (24%) confess to really enjoying shopping for clothes, while one in five (19%) like to keep up with the latest fashions and 13% admit to spending a lot of money on clothes.

'While much has been made about a move away from the metrosexual male back to more "conventional" men, this research shows that the metrosexual man does still have a key part to play in modern Britain,' concludes James McCoy.

About Mintel

Mintel is a worldwide leader of competitive media, product and consumer intelligence. For more than 35 years, Mintel has provided key insight into leading global trends. With offices in Chicago, London, Belfast and Sydney, Mintel's innovative product line provides unique data that has a direct impact on client success. For more information on Mintel, please visit their website at www.mintel.com.
July 2007

⇨ Information from Mintel. Visit www.mintel.com for more information.

© *Mintel*

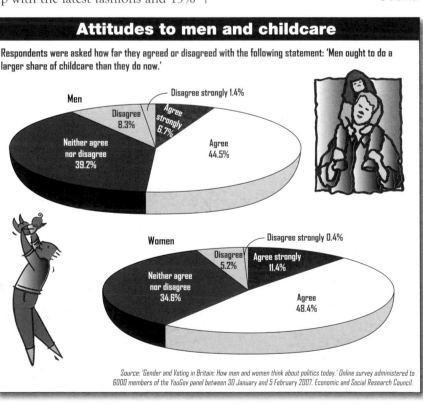

Attitudes to men and childcare

Respondents were asked how far they agreed or disagreed with the following statement: 'Men ought to do a larger share of childcare than they do now.'

Men
- Disagree strongly 1.4%
- Disagree 8.3%
- Agree strongly 6.7%
- Neither agree nor disagree 39.2%
- Agree 44.5%

Women
- Disagree strongly 0.4%
- Disagree 5.2%
- Agree strongly 11.4%
- Neither agree nor disagree 34.6%
- Agree 48.4%

Source: 'Gender and Voting in Britain: How men and women think about politics today.' Online survey administered to 6000 members of the YouGov panel between 30 January and 5 February 2007. Economic and Social Research Council.

Britain and EU failing to mind the gender gap

Household chores condemn women to longer working day. Meanwhile, three-quarters of EU workforce still managed by men

Efforts to reduce the workplace gender gap in Britain and the EU have made little progress since the early 1990s, a Cambridge University report will reveal this week.

The study, the first of its kind since the new EU members joined in 2004, shows that women are still shouldering the bulk of household duties such as cleaning and childcare, meaning that they have significantly longer working days than men.

Academics found a high level of gender segregation in people's working lifestyles, with women generally earning less and struggling to break into senior management roles.

That lifestyle divide, researchers urge, must change if women are to have equal opportunities in the world of work.

'The working lifestyles of most people in Europe still seem to be determined by gender,' said Dr Brendan Burchell, who will present the study in Brussels on Thursday (6 December).

'Gender segregation in employment is pronounced and this widens the gender pay gap. In many cases, we were struck by how little the results for the longer-standing EU nations like Britain, Germany and France have changed since 1991.'

Because women do more work in the home, the report says, they tend to take on more part-time work and lower-paid roles. The greater domestic workload also prevents them from working the long hours typically needed to break into top management jobs.

'That then becomes a vicious circle,' Dr Burchell added. 'Because women are rarely the highest earners in the household, there seems to be an economic rationale for making them responsible for domestic duties. The best way to break that would be to reduce gender inequality in employment and the household together – for instance, by encouraging men to take their parental leave entitlements.'

The report is part of the EU's ongoing European Working Conditions Survey. Door-to-door surveys were carried out in all 27 EU member states, in which over 30,000 employed and self-employed workers were asked to answer questions about their job, their well-being and aspects of their lives outside work. From this, scholars were able to draw up a detailed picture of people's working lives.

They found that three-quarters of the EU workforce are being managed by men, and that just 9% of employed men in full-time work are managed by women. In the UK, women make up just under half the workforce, but they represent less than a third of legislators, managers and senior officials.

Women are also far less likely to have earnings in the highest income bracket. 44% of men working full-time earn a salary deemed 'high', while just 20% of the earnings of women in full-time employment fall into the same category.

Certain types of job also remain heavily dominated by one gender or another. Women remain over-represented in certain services, clerical support jobs and 'caring' professions. Nearly all armed forces personnel, the majority of skilled craft workers, machine operators and senior managers – as well as over half of agricultural and fishery workers – are men.

That in turn leads to different experiences of work for either sex. For instance, women were found to have more office-bound jobs, whereas men are more likely to work from home. Women are significantly more likely to spend at least half their time dealing with people, but also said they found their work more emotionally demanding.

The report also reveals that people in the EU are working harder, but for shorter hours. Once again, the picture is different for men and women. Men spend longer at work, but because of the work they carry out at home, it is women who work more each week if one adds domestic work and paid work together. On average, men in full-time employment work for about 55 hours per week. The average working week for a woman is about 68 hours.

'Because of the expansion of the EU from 15 to 27 this is the first accurate description of gender and working conditions in the enlarged Union,' Dr Burchell added. 'This new report only skims the surface, but it has begun to fill the void. Now that we have published this report giving an overview of the whole EU we can start further analyses of this dataset on a country-by-country basis.

'Our research revealed persistent gender inequalities in many, but not all, types of work and working conditions. If unchecked, the widening of a gender gap in working hours in particular may reduce women's long-term ability to compete with men in the labour market.'

Some other findings from the report

1. 29% of EU27 women are employed part-time compared with 7% of men.
2. Among the professions, the physical, mathematical and engineering sciences are male-dominated, while teaching, the life sciences and health professions are female-dominated.
3. The most heavily male-dominated industrial sector is the construction industry, where men make up 89% of the workforce. The most heavily female-dominated sector is domestic service in private households, where they make up 82% of the workforce.
4. 40% of women employed full-time and 47% of those employed part-time have a female manager.
5. Just over one in five men employed full-time (23%) have some supervisory responsibilities, compared with 15% of women employed full-time.
6. Overall, 38% of employed women provide care for children on a daily basis, 76% cook or do housework

each day and 9% provide care to elderly or disabled relatives every day or every other day.

7. On average, workers in the EU take about 4 and a half days off work every year for health reasons, but there is considerable variety across genders. The average number of days' absence for women is slightly higher than that for men at 5 compared with 4.2. Women full-time workers in professional work stand out with a particularly high number of days' sick leave.

Men spend longer at work, but because of the work they carry out at home, it is women who work more each week if one adds domestic work and paid work together

---

8. The report notes a continued downward trend in working hours in EU12 nations since 1991. The number of part-time workers has risen, although the rise has all but stopped since 2000.
9. 'Overworking' (working for more than 48 hours per week) varies depending on both country and gender. It is most common for men in Romania, Greece, Poland and the Czech Republic. Women are more likely to overwork in Austria, Bulgaria, Greece, Italy, Poland, Romania and Slovenia. In Central Eastern Europe working hours tend to be long for both sexes, with women typically working around 39 or more hours per week, but the average hours for women in Britain or the Netherlands is below 30.
10. Job satisfaction remains high across both genders. Across the EU27, 81% of men and 84% of women reported that they were either satisfied or very satisfied with their job. Working in the UK, Denmark, Sweden, Finland, Ireland, Cyprus or Malta

appears to have a positive impact on recorded job satisfaction, while working in Italy, the Czech Republic, Estonia, Latvia, Lithuania, Hungary, Poland, Slovenia, Slovakia, Bulgaria or Romania appears to have the opposite effect.

11. Both men and women in the EU12 believe they are working at what is referred to as 'high speed' more than 50% of the time, but this is a more marked feature of men's working lives than women's. Across the EU, nearly one in four people contend with high work intensity in their job – but a higher proportion of women have jobs where work intensity is low. Work intensity increased for both men and women in EU15 countries between 1995 and 2005, but the UK has managed to buck this trend, with a decline in the proportion of employees working at high speed or to tight deadlines.

6 December 2007

⇨ The above information is reprinted with kind permission from the University of Cambridge. Visit www.cam.ac.uk for more information.

© University of Cambridge

A bride by any other name

When Eleanor Turner announced that she would not be changing her name after walking down the aisle, and instead her new husband would take on her surname, reactions ranged from shock to annoyance. She considers why breaking with tradition provokes such strong feelings

There are a great many things that make us who we are, and for me one important element is my name. My sisters and I were all named after Queens of England: Alexandra, Eleanor and Victoria, and it was instilled in me from a very early age that my name meant something. My namesake was a proud, powerful woman who lived into a ripe old age and broke all the usual rules of court. A formidable opponent, Queen Eleanor of Aquitaine is still quoted in academic texts as setting the standard in courtly love and scholars write about her with respect and occasionally awe. Growing up in the late 20th century, it was nice for my adolescent self to retain a smug sense of self-righteousness that of all the children in my class, I was the one with the ass-kicking namesake, and to aspire to do it justice in the modern world.

My surname tells a similar tale and thanks to the dedication of my parents and grandparents, it can be traced back to its Welsh and even Scottish roots centuries ago. A fairly common name, Turner, but it still has its history and I'm proud of it. Aside from anything else, it's the name I've had since I was born and it's also the name my husband has now adopted. When we have them, our children will also take my name, and I hope at least some of our grandchildren will too. Does it surprise you then, that I'm a young woman whose beautifully complete family tree does not contain any other examples of husbands taking their wives' names? No, probably not.

At the end of the autumn term last year, I prepared to say my goodbyes to the staff at school for almost a month. I was leaving to get married and have a well-earned break for a honeymoon spent snuggled up in a cosy hotel room with my new husband. A short speech was made by the deputy head and I went up to the front of the room to collect the gift the staff had collected for me. As I stood there, the deputy head asked me: 'So, what will we call you next term?' I answered: 'The same as this term. He's taking my name.' The staff started whooping and I gave them the thumbs up, feeling confident and proud. I then looked at the deputy head again and she looked dismayed, almost as though I'd broken a code. I was soon to find out that a lot of women of all generations felt the same as she did.

For there to be an automatic assumption that I should give up something purely because it's tradition both saddens and frustrates me. Why should I?

The reactions I've had to the decision my husband and I jointly made have been varied and interesting, but always surprising. My sister got married a few months before me and while her husband kept his name, she also kept hers and became a Ms. The most eye-blinking reaction came from our mother, who upon being informed of her daughters' separate-yet-similar decisions, told us we were being selfish, as this would mess up the family tree down the line. Our aunt also told us that it was better to stick to traditional setups as this causes less confusion for other people, including children. My husband's mother even went as far as to be cross with me - after all, she'd had to adopt the Schmitt family name, so why couldn't I?

My husband is the eldest of four healthy, virile and heterosexual sons who will all, no doubt, marry and produce litters of offspring with their wives. I am the middle child of three daughters, one of whom is mentally disabled and will never marry. My in-laws' name will therefore no doubt continue into the 21st century, whereas mine is less assured. My husband and I discussed our future married name thoughtfully and frequently, and came to the following conclusions: a) four sons vs. three daughters, b) he likes my name, I'm not so keen on his, c) we want one family name and d) we're a partnership and will make joint decisions that are right for our marriage.

My personal argument? It's my name, my choice. My children can do whatever they like with their names, as long as any decision they make is a mature and consensual one made with their partner. Marriage is a partnership. It is a binding decision to spend the rest of your life with

one person and share everything with them. The foundation block of this is becoming one unit with one surname and I really don't see what the problem is. My husband and I share everything – housework, wages, financial obligations – even the driving. For there to be an automatic assumption, therefore, that I should give up something purely because it's tradition both saddens and frustrates me. Why should I?

Now, it's all well and good saying a name is changing, but the practicalities of carrying out such a task are more complex, particularly if you're male. If I had become Mrs Schmitt, all I'd have to do is send off my marriage certificate to the passport office, credit card people, the bank and mortgage lenders and the change would be immediate. If, however, you're a man and becoming Mr Turner, you have to change it by deed poll. This costs money and a considerable amount of time. Even though we've been married for three months, because my husband is American his name is still officially Schmitt. The whole system promotes inequality – men have to jump through hoops to change their names after marriage, but if you're a woman, welcome to the bandwagon! You'll notice that there are no spaces for 'master name' in place of 'maiden' on these forms so I'm proposing a blanket rule. One generic term for men and women called 'previous name' under that all important Personal Details section, and the opportunity for all agencies and institutions to allow men to change their details and marriage status as easily as women.

One argument against couples reaching mutual decisions about their family name is that society is traditionally a patriarchy, and names and property are carried down the male line. I'd like to challenge this. Ever since women won the hard-fought fight to be allowed to vote, divorce and keep their own property, male-heir dynasties should have been outlawed. So what if family trees become more difficult to trace? If that's the argument perhaps we should all convert to having our mothers' names. We did literally come from their bodies, after all. Are we more their property than our fathers'?

There do exist some matriarchies in the world, and academics will always find and quote from some remote African tribe where the men lead solitary, roaming lives and the women look after the babies. It makes more sense to have a matriarch in charge and to take the female line's name as the fathers are off doing their thing and very rarely around. Now, aside from the very obvious issues one may have with this setup (Why are the women bringing up their babies by themselves? Don't children need two parents? Oh, don't get me started on the effect absent fathers has on the teenagers at my school), the fact is, in the vast majority of the various and colourful societies of this world, patriarchy is the norm, and so is the expectation that women will conform to its traditions. After making my announcement at school, I had so many visits from both male and female staff asking me how I had 'convinced' my husband to take my name and how both his and my

parents felt about it. It says a lot that my colleagues were more interested in the effect my 'manipulation' had on the men in my life than congratulating me and my partner for treading a path less trod.

I think that the decision Mike and I made, and the name we had read out to us in our church wedding, has really offended some of the people I've spoken to. Some people seem to take it as a personal insult, almost as though I am saying that the decision they made to follow an outdated tradition was the wrong one. A part of me wonders if there is actually an underlying jealousy about, as people (namely women) wish they'd thought of it first. Another part of me is hoping that I am challenging people's beliefs and however small an effect it may be having; at least it's having one. And that's the thing, isn't it? Small changes lead to big ones, and if I can convince one other young woman to simply talk to her partner about their future married name rather than comply with tradition, it'll be a job well done.

About the author

Eleanor Turner is currently attempting to decide her master's degree programme and slowly opening her eyes to the inequalities of the world, one feminist author at a time.
2 May 2007

⇨ The above information is reprinted with kind permission from Eleanor Turner and The F Word, featuring articles on contemporary feminism. Visit www.thefword.org.uk for more.
© Eleanor Turner

Equality is the way to a woman's heart

New polling published today finds that equality is the way to a woman's heart (and her vote)

In a report published today by the Fawcett Society, research funded by the ESRC and analysed by academics Rosie Campbell and Kristi Winters reveals that women want greater equality at home, at work and in politics.

Equality at home

Today's poll reveals that pressure is building for men to do a greater share of childcare and housework. The poll suggests that men seeking the perfect Valentine's Day treat would be better advised to abandon the traditional bunch of roses in favour of changing nappies and picking up the duster.

The poll finds that the majority of both women and men think that men should do more childcare. But, what about men taking a fair share of the housework? The poll shows that a greater percentage of women want men to be more active around the house – 69% of women think that men should do more housework compared to 56% of men.

Equality in politics

And, women's concern with equality is not confined to the domestic sphere. Women's political values are more pro-equality and they are looking to Government to do more to promote women's chances.

More than a third (35%) of women think that attempts to ensure equality for women have not gone far enough (compared to 18% of men) and more women express a desire to be represented by women MPs.

Responding to today's survey, Dr Rosie Campbell, Lecturer at Birkbeck College, University of London, said:

'This survey shows us that on a number of issues women's political values are to the left of men's. Women are more concerned about inequality and are slightly less tolerant

of poverty than men. Women want greater equality in the home and in society. Women still feel that attempts to bring about equality for women haven't gone far enough and politicians have more work to do.'

Katherine Rake, Director of the Fawcett Society, said:

'Published on Valentine's Day, this poll reminds us that equality is a more effective way to women's hearts than a bunch of roses or a candlelit dinner. Women have experienced a revolution in their working lives over the past 30 years. What is clear from today's report is that they now expect men to undergo a similar revolution and fully share with them the responsibility for family and home.

'Politicians too need to sit up and take note if they are to appeal to women voters. Women are looking for a new type of politics which reflects women's greater commitment to equality generally and their desire to see more done on women's equality.'

Key findings from the survey include:

⇨ 69% of women and 56% of men felt that men should do more housework than they do now.

⇨ 60% of women and 51% of men felt that men should do more childcare than they do now.

⇨ 27% of women and 21% of men felt that women MPs better represent the interests of women.

⇨ 35% of women and 18% of men felt that attempts to ensure equality for women had not gone far enough.

⇨ 84% of women and 80% of men felt that the gap between the rich and poor was too large.

⇨ 58% of women and 51% of men

Pressure is building for men to do a greater share of childcare and housework

felt that one of the biggest problems in Britain is that not everyone is given an equal chance to succeed.

⇨ 71% of women and 63% of men felt that ordinary working people don't get a fair share of the nation's wealth.

⇨ 35% of women and 30% of men would like to see taxes raised and spent on health, education and social services.

⇨ 56% of women and 35% of men felt that censorship of films and magazines is necessary to uphold moral values.

The survey was administered to 6000 members of the YouGov panel between 30 January and 5 February 2007. The data are weighted according to YouGov's procedure. In total 2890 people responded to the survey. This report is one output of a larger research project, the details of which can be found at http://www.bbk.ac.uk/polsoc/research/rcampbellvoting
14 February 2007

⇨ The above information is reprinted with kind permission from the Fawcett Society. Visit www.fawcettsociety.org.uk for more information.

nd education

⇨ l
va
reco
Stage
internatic   .rent
results) sho   .der gap
is wide in Eı.   .ınd narrower
in Maths, with, on average, girls
performing better than boys. The
gender gap in the Sciences has
been traditionally very small.

GCSE attainment

There has been a long-standing
gender gap at GCSE for those
attaining 5+ A*-C:

⇨ Since 1988, on the threshold
measure of 5+ A-C GCSEs, a
significant gender gap in favour of
girls has emerged. This gap quickly
increased and subsequently
became stable at around a 10
percentage points difference,
with little variation since 1995.
The gender gap is currently 9.6
percentage points: 63.4 per cent
of girls and 53.8 per cent of boys
achieved 5+ A*-C GCSEs or
equivalent in 2006.

Girls tend to do better in the
majority of GCSE subjects:

⇨ The largest gender differences
(a female advantage of more
than ten percentage points on
those gaining an A*-C GCSE)
are for the Humanities, the Arts
and Languages. Smaller gender
differences (a female advantage
of five percentage points or less)
tend to be in Science and Maths
subjects.

⇨ Some of these achievement
patterns have been relatively stable
over six decades of exam results,
particularly in English Language
and Literature, French, Art and
Design and Religious Studies.

n changing patterns
ears. In Maths, there has
a shift from a male advantage
.veraging 4 percentage points prior
to 1991 to a slim female advantage
of 1-2 percentage points in recent
years. In Geography, there has
been a widening of the gap in girls'
favour, and in History, there has
been fluctuation but with girls
now doing much better than boys.

Girls are more likely than boys to gain an A* grade at GCSE

⇨ Attainment at each end of the
distribution of grades also varies
by gender. Girls are more likely
than boys to gain an A* grade at
GCSE. Boys are a little more likely
to gain a G grade at GCSE or to
gain no GCSEs at all.

GCSE subject choice

There are important gender differences
in subject choices:

⇨ Taking the ten most popular
GCSE choices, nine out of ten
subjects are chosen by both boys
and girls. Nonetheless, many
subjects show gender-stereotypical
biases with girls more likely to take
Arts, Languages and Humanities
and boys more likely to take Geography, Physical Education and IT.

A-level entries and subject choice

Post-16 participation rates vary by
gender:

⇨ Girls are more likely to stay on in
full-time education at age 16 (82
per cent of girls and 72 per cent of
boys). Girls are also more likely to
be entered for A-levels than boys

(54 per cent of entries are female),
in contrast to the 1950s and 1960s
when only a third of A-level entries
were female.

Gender differences in subject choice
become more accentuated post-16:

⇨ Gender differences in subject
choice are greater at A-level than
at GCSE. Girls' most popular
subject is English, while boys' is
Maths. Psychology, Art and Design,
Sociology and Media/Film/
Television Studies are amongst
the ten most popular choices for
girls (but not boys), while Physics,
Business Studies, Geography and
Physical Education are in the top
ten for boys (but not girls).

⇨ Girls' participation in Physics is
particularly low and is the least
popular of the three Sciences,
accounting for only 1.3 per cent
of female A-level entries. For boys,

Physics remains the most popular science but whereas it used to be the most popular subject overall, it now is in sixth place and represents only 5.7 per cent of male entries.

A-level attainment

Gender differences in pass rate are much narrower at A-level than at GCSE but gender differences still exist:

⇨ Across all subjects, the range of difference is 4 percentage points. This is in the context of a very high pass rate.

⇨ Girls perform better than boys in terms of those attaining an A grade (for the majority of subjects), which is a significant change over the last ten years.

Foundation Stage and Key Stage 1–3 results

Gender patterns remain relatively stable when looking at attainment in English, Maths and Science across different stages of compulsory education:

⇨ There is a gender gap in English from the Foundation Stage through to GCSE. Although the gender gap is largest at Key Stages 3 and 4, girls and boys do not make dramatically different progress between Key Stages.

⇨ The gender gap in Maths is smaller than English but girls are performing slightly better than boys at Foundation Stage, and at Key Stages 1, 3 and 4.

⇨ Gender differences in Science are relatively small.

International evidence

Evidence from international research shows similar patterns:

⇨ International evidence for the PISA study (Programme for International Student Assessment) covering countries in the OECD (Organisation for Economic Co-operation and Development) and their partners, shows that girls have significantly better reading scores than boys in all participating countries (except Liechtenstein).

⇨ For Maths, boys were significantly ahead of girls in half the participating countries (but the

difference was smaller than for reading), while in the other half, there was no significant difference.

⇨ In Science, there were no systematic gender differences.

⇨ The size of the gender gap does, however, vary between countries. Looking at the gender gap for England, the findings show that there was no statistical difference between boys and girls in Maths. Alongside the majority of countries, the gender gap in literacy was statistically significant for England but was smaller than the OECD average.

The PISA study has also highlighted differing trends in learning style:

⇨ Girls are more likely than boys to control their learning (i.e. review what they have learned; review what they still need to learn) in all but four OECD countries.

⇨ There are also contrasting gender differences in measures of motivation. In most countries, girls claim more effort and persistence and express significantly greater interest in reading. Boys show significantly more interest in Maths in most countries – by small degrees in some countries, but by much more in others.

Gender, social class and ethnicity

Gender is not the strongest predictor of attainment:

⇨ The social class attainment gap at Key Stage 4 (as measured by percentage point difference in attainment between those eligible and not eligible for free school meals [FSM]) is three times as wide as the gender gap.

⇨ Some minority ethnic groups attain significantly below the national average and their under-achievement is much greater than the gap between boys and girls.

Nonetheless, gender is an in-dependent and significant predictor of attainment:

⇨ The gap in attainment at GCSE between boys and girls is relatively stable across the social class groupings i.e. the effect of gender does not systematically vary to any great extent across social class.

⇨ However, the gender gap at GCSE does seem to vary by ethnic group, with Black Caribbean and Black Other pupils having wider gender gaps than other ethnic groups. In particular, Black Caribbean and Black Other boys are the least likely of any ethnic group to achieve 5+ A*-C GCSE passes, but Black Caribbean and Black Other girls are not disadvantaged to the same extent.

White British FSM boys are a group with particularly low attainment:

⇨ Only 24 per cent gain 5+ A*-C GCSEs (33 percentage points less well than average attainment at GCSE).

⇨ However, White British FSM boys are not the only group with low attainment. Black Caribbean FSM boys and White British FSM girls are also doing significantly less well than the national average (respectively, 30 and 26 percentage points less well than average attainment at GCSE).

⇨ In addition, the attainment of Black Caribbean non-FSM boys is well below the average (18 percentage points lower). The reasons for these groups' lower attainment are poorly understood but for each group, a different combination of factors (with gender playing a role) may be of relevance.

Therefore, consideration of social class and ethnicity alongside gender helps to identify which children are 'underachieving':

⇨ The analyses show that labelling boys as 'underachieving' is too broad-brush, but highlighting White British FSM boys as 'underachieving' (because they are a large group with the lowest attainment at GCSE, apart from traveller groups) risks losing sight of other poor performing children.

Assessing the gender gap

There are three main caveats about the gender gap:

⇨ The gender gap arises mainly because of differences between boys and girls in language and lit-eracy skills, reflected in differences in performance in English and other subjects which are literacy based. The gender gap is small or negligible for Maths and Science. These trends are apparent both from historical data from English exam records going back 60 years and from international data.

⇨ While gender does independently predict attainment, the social class gap has greater explanatory power and for some groups, ethnicity is also a more important factor than gender.

⇨ A focus on boys' underachievement can shift attention away from the fact that large numbers of girls are also low attainers. Tackling the scale of these numbers is arguably of greater priority and importance to policy makers than the proportionate difference between boys' and girls' attainment. Additionally, the different subject choices made by boys and girls may be more marked and have greater longer-term outcomes in terms of subsequent career choices than attainment differences.

Cognitive differences

⇨ In contrast to national assessments, small or negligible overall gender differences have been found on IQ tests and tests of reasoning. The relatively small gender differences detected in verbal reasoning do not seem to predict the large gender differences found in English and other humanity subjects in National Curriculum Assessments.

Pre-school differences

Pre-school gender differences in social, cognitive and communication measures have been found, as well as gender differences in the activities that parents carry out with their children:

⇨ Data from the Millennium Cohort Study suggest gender differences are apparent in early communicative gestures at 9 months old, with, for example, female infants more likely to wave goodbye. However, for the majority of developmental measures considered, small or negligible gender differences were found.

⇨ At the pre-school stage, girls have better social and cognitive skills.

⇨ Parents are more likely to read and teach songs and nursery rhymes with their daughters than their sons.

⇨ Pre-school provision helped boost boys' early number concepts but had no differential impact on early literacy skills.

Gender and Special Educational Needs

Boys are more likely than girls to be identified with special educational needs:

⇨ Seventy per cent of children with identified SEN are boys.

⇨ Boys are more likely than girls to attend special schools.

⇨ Boys are nine times as likely as girls to be identified with autistic spectrum disorder.

⇨ Boys are four times as likely as

girls to be identified as having a behavioural, emotional and social difficulty (BESD).

⇨ Gender is a better predictor than social class and ethnicity of being classified as having BESD.

⇨ Boys from Black Caribbean, White/Black Caribbean and any Other Black background are proportionately more likely to be identified with BESD.

Gender and behaviour

There appear to be no gender differences in pupils' attitudes towards school but there are important gender differences in boys' and girls' behaviour. There is evidence that boys and girls who become disaffected tend to take different pathways.

Concerning exclusions from school:

⇨ Boys account for 80 per cent of permanent exclusions and three-quarters of fixed term exclusions.

⇨ There has been an increase in the proportion of girls receiving permanent exclusions over the last seven years: in 1998, girls accounted for 16 per cent of permanent exclusions; 2005 figures show that they now account for 21 per cent of permanent exclusions. This is due to a decline in the percentage of boys receiving exclusions while the percentage of girls receiving exclusions has remained relatively stable.

⇨ There is little variation in the exclusion rates of boys and girls across ethnic groups. Boys from White, Black and Mixed backgrounds are excluded (both fixed term and permanent) at approximately 2.6-3.5 times the rate of girls. The gender disparity for Asian pupils is slightly larger than average, though overall rates are low.

⇨ FSM pupils are three times more likely to receive an exclusion (fixed period or permanent) than non-FSM pupils. The increased rate is similar for both FSM boys and FSM girls. As boys overall have a higher rate of exclusions, the rate for FSM boys is high: the proportion of fixed period exclusions is 18 per cent for FSM

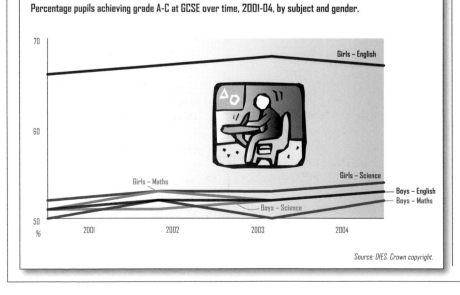

GCSE achievement over time

Percentage pupils achieving grade A-C at GCSE over time, 2001-04, by subject and gender.

Girls – English
Girls – Maths
Girls – Science
Boys – English
Boys – Maths
Boys – Science

Source: DfES. Crown copyright.

boys compared to 7 per cent for non-FSM boys. The comparable figures for girls are 6 per cent (FSM girls) and 2 per cent (non-FSM girls).

Concerning absence rates:

⇨ Girls have slightly higher rates of authorised absence than boys but there are no gender differences in unauthorised absence.

⇨ Higher than average levels of absence (authorised and/or unauthorised) are associated with reduced attainment at Key Stage 3 and GCSE, with a particular impact on boys.

Concerning bullying:

⇨ Girls are more likely than boys to have been the victim of psychological bullying while boys are more likely than girls to have been the victim of physical bullying.

Concerning youth offending:

⇨ Boys are more likely to have committed a criminal offence (e.g. handling stolen goods, stealing, carrying a weapon) than girls (33 per cent compared to 21 per cent).

Reasons for the gender gap

The literature on the reasons behind the gender gap reveals a complex story:

⇨ Girls and boys tend to use different styles of learning. Girls tend to show greater levels of motivation and respond differently to the materials and tasks given to them.

⇨ Overall trends indicate that girls and boys seem to relate differently to schooling and learning and girls find it easier to succeed in school settings.

⇨ Type of school does not appear to influence the gender gap: across schools in England, there are hardly any where boys make greater progress than girls.

⇨ However, one study found that there are a large proportion of schools where boys and girls make similar progress but these tend to be schools where school performance is weak (i.e. for both boys and girls). The corollary of this is that the gender gap is wider in better performing schools.

⇨ Boys are more likely to be influenced by their male peer group which might devalue schoolwork and so put them at odds with academic achievement.

⇨ A recent study found that the introduction of the National Literacy and Numeracy Strategies had an impact on the gender gap by improving the attainment of boys (more than girls) in English, and girls (more than boys) in Maths. However, the gap persists.

⇨ The use of coursework in examinations may advantage girls but analysis does not find that this alone accounts for the gender gap.

⇨ Other aspects of the curriculum, assessment structure and content have also been implicated. For example, reading assessments which focus on narrative may accentuate the gender gap compared to more factual-based assessment. A study has shown that boys performed significantly better on a reading comprehension task involving factual content compared to one based on narrative content. Girls' reading comprehension scores were less influenced by the content of the task.

Raising attainment

Research indicates that:

⇨ Combating images of laddish masculinity and establishing a strong school ethos were seen as central to raising the attainment of boys. In order for specific strategies to be successful, pupils with this sort of self-image need to be offered support and their achievements valued.

⇨ Strategies to raise boys' achievement, if successful, are also likely to raise girls' achievement, and thus perpetuate the gender gap. It has been argued that any strategy to raise boys' achievement should not be done in a way that could be detrimental to girls' social or academic progress.

⇨ There is not a case for boy-friendly pedagogies – pedagogies which appeal to and engage boys are equally girl-friendly.

Single-sex education

The 'jury is still out' on the impact of single-sex schooling on educational attainment:

⇨ Several international reviews and systematic reviews have failed to identify consistent or strong findings for the impact of single-sex education.

⇨ That said, there is some evidence that girls' and boys' attitudes to subjects are influenced by whether a pupil attends a single-sex school. Boys and girls attending single-sex schools are less likely to hold gender-stereotypical views about science subjects compared to pupils attending co-educational schools.

School workforce

There are marked gender differences in the school workforce at primary level, but less so at secondary level:

⇨ The majority of teachers in nursery and primary schools are female (84 per cent) and this pattern has become increasingly accentuated over the years.

⇨ The gender split at secondary is more even, with 56 per cent of teachers being female. This represents a significant change: prior to 1993, a greater proportion of teachers were male than female.

⇨ Men are more likely to get promoted to headship. While only 16 per cent of nursery/primary school teachers are male, 34 per cent of head teachers are male. While only 44 per cent of secondary school teachers are male, 65 per cent of head teachers are male. However, the proportion of female head teachers has increased in recent years.

⇨ It has been hypothesised that the gender mix of teachers could play a role in the observed gender gap in attainment but this is difficult to measure and there is no strong evidence to date that this is the case.

⇨ The above information is reprinted with kind permission from the Department for Children, Schools and Families. Visit www.dcsf.gov.uk for more information.

Gender and subject choice

Information from the Department for Children, Schools and Families

⇨ While girls are now achieving better academic results than boys at age 16, relatively few young women are choosing science or science-related subjects for further study.

⇨ Boys dominate in maths, science and technology at A-level and far more men than women study these subjects in higher education. This has significant implications for men's and women's career choices and future earnings: 60% of working women are clustered in only 10% of occupations; and men are also under-represented in a number of occupations.

Relatively few young women are choosing science or science-related subjects for further study

⇨ Pupils' subject and course choices are influenced by a range of factors: their own views and expectations, those of their peers, parents and teachers, and the media.
  Some words of warning:

⇨ Most single-sex girls' schools are in the Independent sector; this makes for difficult comparisons with a national picture, as it is likely that any differences are artefacts of the Independent/ Maintained split rather than the gender difference.

⇨ Although the list of subjects above attempts to classify what are traditionally 'feminine' areas of the curriculum, in today's world, such stereotyping is difficult to pin down – is, for example, medicine a 'traditionally' masculine career choice? 30 years ago, this might have been true, but it could be argued that it is no longer the case.

⇨ There is a problem over deciding what is 'choice' in terms of a school system (i.e. the choices pupils make for subjects studied). At GCSE there is still some restriction (both in terms of curriculum requirement and what the school opts for en bloc or by being a Specialist School), and it could be argued that only in a post-16 environment is there a true measure of 'choice'.

⇨ The above information is re-printed with kind permission from the Department for Children, Schools and Families. Visit www.dcsf.gov.uk for more information.

© Crown copyright

Boys and single-sex teaching

Boys need to be taught separately from the age of five, says expert. By Sarah Harris

Boys need to be taught separately from girls from the age of five to prevent them being damaged by the education system, an expert claimed yesterday.

Dr Leonard Sax argues that boys are 'turned off' by starting formal education too soon when they are expected to sit down and keep quiet in class.

And, because they develop at different rates to girls, they can be discouraged from learning while very young when sat alongside female classmates.

Dr Sax, a research psychologist in the US, claims this has led to an epidemic of unmotivated boys and under-achieving young men.

He said: 'With boys you have to start right away. If you wait until secondary school, you have waited too long. From the age of five, there are clear advantages in all-boys education when teachers know how to take advantage of it.'

He believes girls also benefit from single-sex education because they can concentrate on subjects such as maths, which is traditionally seen as a 'male' interest.

At present, single-sex education is concentrated in the independent sector. Dr Sax wants more state primary and secondary schools to offer single-sex classes.

He added: 'Boys' and girls' brains develop along profoundly different timetables.

'It might be appropriate to ask five-year-old girls to sit still and be quiet in class, but for many five-year-old boys it is not developmentally appropriate.

'The message they get at five is that doing well in school is something that girls do.'

Young boys become afraid of being seen as 'swots'. However, in single-sex classes they are more likely to see getting good grades as 'cool'.

Dr Sax, the author of a new book, *Boys Adrift*, argues that boys are suffering a 'toxic' mix of failing to be engaged by the curriculum, overuse of video games, lack of competitive sport at school and over-prescription of attention disorder drugs.

He said: 'The video game world is more real to them than the world of homework and grades.'

He suggested parents limit the amount of time boys spend playing these games to no more than 40 minutes on school days.

⇨ This article first appeared in the *Daily Mail*, 23 January 2008.

© 2008 Associated Newspapers Ltd

The myth of single-sex schooling

New research dispels myths surrounding single-sex schooling

A study of people now in their 40s has revealed that those who went to single-sex schools were more likely to study subjects not traditionally associated with their gender than those who went to co-educational schools. Girls from single-sex schools also went on to earn more than those from co-educational schools.

The research, by the Institute of Education's Centre for Longitudinal Studies, has followed almost 13,000 individuals born in 1958 throughout their lives and so can tell us about longer-term consequences of types of schools.

The researchers found that at age 16, girls in girls' schools were more likely to gain maths and science A-levels, and boys in boys' schools more liable to gain A-levels in English and modern languages than their peers in co-educational schools. Girls and boys in single-sex schools also had more confidence in their ability to do well in these subjects.

The pattern carried through to university, with women from girls' schools more likely than co-educated women to gain qualifications in subjects typically dominated by men and to go on to earn higher salaries in their jobs.

Researcher Dr Alice Sullivan explains: 'Single-sex schools seemed more likely to encourage students to pursue academic paths according to their talents rather than their gender, whereas more gender-stereotyped choices were made in co-educational schools. This suggests that co-educational schools need to examine the ways in which they have, probably unwittingly, enforced powerful gender stereotypes on both girls and boys.'

Researcher Professor Diana Leonard says: 'Although having been to a single-sex school is not significantly linked to a gender atypical occupation, girls from single-sex schools do get higher wages in later life. This could be because they are carrying out more technical or scientific roles even within female-dominated jobs, for example, becoming science teachers rather than French teachers, or because they have learned to be more self-confident in negotiating their wages and salaries.'

> **Women from girls' schools were more likely than co-educated women to gain qualifications in subjects typically dominated by men and to go on to earn higher salaries**

But single-sex education brought almost no advantage in terms of exam results. Girls from girls' schools did only slightly better in exams than their co-educational peers. Boys did no better at all (allowing for differences in ability and family background). While girls at girls' schools were slightly more likely than girls in mixed schools to gain five or more O-levels at grades A-C, this advantage did not carry through to further and higher education. There was no impact of single-sex schooling on maths test scores at age 16, nor did single-sex schooling make it more likely for pupils to gain any A-levels at all, to get a university degree by age 33, or to enter high-status occupations.

Dr Sullivan says: 'Our research emphatically does not support the suggestion that achievement is higher in single-sex schools.'

Other findings showed that boys in boys' schools were more likely to dislike school than boys in co-ed schools, but both sexes were less likely to truant in single-sex schools.

Single-sex schooling appeared to have no impact on the likelihood of marriage or childbearing, or on the quality of partnerships formed. Neither did it appear to affect the division of labour in the home, nor attitudes to women's work outside the home. However, men who had attended single-sex schools were more likely to be divorced by age 42.

This research was funded by the Economic and Social Research Council. A version of this Working Paper will be published in: Scott, J., Dex, S. and Joshi, H. (eds) (forthcoming 2008) Changing patterns of women's employment over 25 years. Cheltenham: Edward Elgar.

19 September 2006

⇨ The above information is reprinted with kind permission from the Centre for Longitudinal Studies. Visit www.cls.ioe.ac.uk for more information.

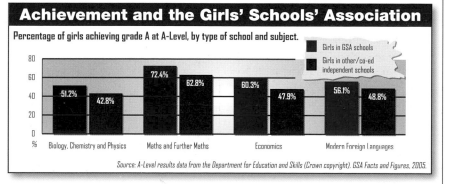

Achievement and the Girls' Schools' Association

Percentage of girls achieving grade A at A-Level, by type of school and subject.

Legend: Girls in GSA schools / Girls in other/co-ed independent schools

- Biology, Chemistry and Physics: 51.2% / 42.8%
- Maths and Further Maths: 72.4% / 62.8%
- Economics: 60.3% / 47.9%
- Modern Foreign Languages: 56.1% / 48.8%

Source: A-Level results data from the Department for Education and Skills (Crown copyright). GSA Facts and Figures, 2005.

Gender bias still blights school careers advice

Girlguiding UK members say guidance reinforces job stereotypes

⇨ *One in three girls and young women says gender influenced careers advice.*

⇨ *Only one in five was encouraged to pursue a traditionally 'male' career.*

⇨ *Less than one in three got enough information on the pay implications of career choices.*

New research published by Girlguiding UK today has revealed that careers advice for young women remains strongly prejudiced by gender. The survey showed 35% of Senior Section members aged 14-26 believe being female has influenced the types of careers they are encouraged to follow.

Nearly two-thirds of the girls aged 16-17 yrs (62%) thought there was not enough information about how much you could expect to be paid in different careers, rising to 85% among those aged 22-26 yrs.

The findings suggest modern careers advice continues to affirm old-fashioned gender stereotypes. Girls say they are twice as likely to be actively encouraged to pursue more traditional female careers (34%) such as teaching and childcare as to be directed towards new opportunities in jobs that tend to be associated with their male counterparts (18%).

Over three-quarters of girls said the reasons young women are deterred from entering male-dominated professions are largely down to lack of proper information (78%). Over two-thirds said girls tend to be concerned about possible discrimination from colleagues (69%) or from employers (68%). A lack of positive role models working in what are perceived to be traditionally male environments was also mentioned by 68%.

In choosing future careers nearly six in ten girls (57%) received information about going into teaching and over two-fifths (43%) about working in childcare. Conversely less than a third were told about the opportunities to work in IT (29%) or business and entrepreneurship (28%), only a fifth were informed about engineering (21%) and fewer than one in ten received enough information about construction (9%) or plumbing (6%).

Two-thirds of 16- and 17-year-olds (67%) and three-quarters of 22- to 26-year-olds (76%) thought careers advice was not given enough time in school timetables. Only half thought they were given enough information at the critical time of choosing courses leading to qualifications such as GCSEs (46%). Only a third of 22- to 26-year-olds (30%) felt the advice they received on a range of career choices was up-to-date, though information appears to be improving for the 16- and 17-year-olds, almost half of whom (46%) said their careers information was current.

The good news is that more than nine in ten girls thought providing equal careers advice for both sexes could be achieved through better training for teachers and careers advisers (95%). There was an equally strong call for better information on where to go for advice and support (89%) and more non-traditional work experience opportunities (87%).

Activities undertaken through Girlguiding UK were the main influence on career choices with one in five girls saying these activities had a direct impact on the jobs they would like to have (20%), followed by work experience placements (16%), parents (15%), teachers/careers advisers (15%) and friends (3%).

Careers advice for young women remains strongly prejudiced by gender

Chief Guide Liz Burnley said: 'These outdated gender barriers must be broken down so young women can determine their own successful career paths. Our young members are calling for better information, support and guidance about career options so they can make informed decisions about their futures. At Girlguiding UK we're delighted to see the positive impact we've had on girls' career choices and we will continue to help girls develop the necessary skills to achieve their goals in the modern world of work.'

Comments from the girls and young women surveyed include:

'I only had one 20-minute session with the adviser in seven years of secondary school.'

'Traditionally male industries should come and talk to boys and girls separately so neither feel pressure or embarrassed by the other sex.'

'I feel that I have been pushed by teachers and career advisers to pursue a traditional female line of work, for example childcare or hairdressing. The opportunity to discuss other options was never presented.'
14 August 2007

⇨ The above information is reprinted with kind permission from The Guide Association. Visit www.girlguiding.org.uk for more information.
© *The Guide Association 2007*

Women and work: the facts

Information from Opportunity Now

Achieving gender equality and diversity within the workplace is good for business, good for women and good for society.

Good for business

Increasing women's participation in the labour market and reducing gender segregation in the workplace is estimated to be worth between £15 billion and £23 billion to the UK economy. There are a number of studies that show a link between gender distribution in a company's management and its profitability. Research from Catalyst in the USA shows companies with the highest representation of women on their top management teams delivered 35.1% higher return on equity, and 34% higher total return to shareholders than companies with the lowest representation.

Achievements

Women in the workforce

⇨ 46.7% of the UK labour force is female.

⇨ Out of the 27 European Union countries, the UK has the fourth highest employment rate for women, after The Netherlands, Finland, and Estonia.

Women have the skills employers need

⇨ 63.4% of girls and 53.8% of boys achieve 5 or more GCSEs grades A*-C.

⇨ 56.6% is the proportion of first degrees that are obtained by women.

opportunity**now**
men | women | workplace

Women are achieving the most senior positions

⇨ 28% of all directors are women.

⇨ 11% of FTSE 100 directorships are held by women.

⇨ 27.5% of the civil service top management are women.

⇨ 21.2% of local government chief executives are women.

⇨ 18.7% of all judges are women.

⇨ 9% of police officers ranked as chief constable, deputy chief constable or assistant chief constable are women.

⇨ 16% of vice-chancellors are women.

Taking action on gender diversity can increase customer base

⇨ 80% is the proportion of consumer buying decisions made by women.

⇨ £60 billion is the amount contributed to the UK economy by women-owned businesses.

⇨ £100 billion is the annual spend of the public sector on procuring goods and services. All public authorities require that suppliers fulfil the obligations of the Gender Equality Duty.

Diversity

Women are diverse. Understanding the multiple layers of identity will enable employers to reach under-utilised pools of talent.

Age

The labour force is ageing. One in five people in the world will be over 60 by 2050, compared to one in twelve in 1950. But employers are still underutilising older workers, particularly women. The employment rate of men in the UK aged 50 and over was 44% in 2004; for women it was 31%. The European objective is to raise this to 50%.

Disability

Just 50% of the 3.5 million disabled women of working age in the UK are in employment.

Ethnicity

At 7.9% from a non-white ethnic group the UK population is becoming more diverse. Yet many ethnic minority women remain outside the labour market. The employment rate is highest for white British women at 73%; it is lowest for Pakistani women at just 28%.

Mothers

At 71% the employment rate for mothers who are married or co-habiting is just slightly less than that of women without dependent children (73%).

The employment rate for lone mothers is considerably lower at 56%.

Mothers (who are married or co-habiting) are twice as likely to work part-time (41%) compared with women without dependent children, (22% work part-time).

Religion

Over 1.5 million women in the UK hold a religion other than Christianity; around half of these are Muslim.

Economic inactivity is greatest amongst Muslim women at 69%.

Sexual orientation

6% of the population is gay.

Transgender

It is estimated that rates of transexuality are 1 in 10,000 men and 1 in 40,000 women.

Where women work

Six out of ten workers in the UK's private sector are male, while women dominate in the public sector (65%) research has found.

The *Economic & Labour Market Review*, published by the Office for National Statistics in 2007, found that the number of female workers in the public sector has only increased

2% from 63% in 1997, while in the private sector, the proportion of men and women has remained stable over the past decade.

According to the latest statistics, 31% of male private sector workers clocked up 45-hour weeks, against 22% of their counterparts in the public sector. For women, only 10% in the public sector and 9% of private sector women worked 45-hour weeks.

Female employment is concentrated within the services sector and within administrative and service occupations.

Sectors with the highest proportion of jobs held by women

⇨ Education, health and public admin: 70%
⇨ Distribution, hotels and catering: 51%
⇨ Other services: 50%

Sectors with the lowest proportion of jobs held by women

⇨ Energy and water: 24%
⇨ Transport and communications: 24%
⇨ Construction: 10%

Occupations with the highest proportion of jobs held by women

⇨ Personal services: 83%
⇨ Admin and secretarial: 78%
⇨ Sales and customer services: 69%

Occupations with the lowest proportion of jobs held by women

⇨ Managers and senior officials: 35%
⇨ Process plant and machine operatives: 14%
⇨ Skilled trades: 8%

Challenges

Skills

The skills of many women are under-utilised.

⇨ 50% of women working in low-paid part-time jobs are working beneath their potential, i.e. they are not using their skills, experience or qualifications for their current job.
⇨ Two-thirds of the half a million women in the UK qualified in science, engineering or technology (SET) do not work in those sectors.
⇨ In 2005 women represented 50% of rural employees. There is no single initiative to help rural women enter the labour market although 40% of rural women of working age not in paid employment have said they would like to do so.

Pay

From the age of 18 women receive less pay than men in every occupational group.

⇨ 44,013 is the number of equal pay claims brought between April 2006 and April 2007.
⇨ £60 million is the estimated cost of the UK's largest equal pay award. North Cumbria NHS Trust paid an average of £40,000 to 1500 women who had been underpaid.
⇨ Out of the 27 European Union countries, the UK has the largest pay gap.
⇨ 82.8p is the amount a woman earns for every pound that a man earns, the equivalent to working in November and December every year for free!
⇨ 64.4p is the amount a woman working part-time earns for every pound paid to the average man.

Sex discrimination

Women experience discrimination at work.

⇨ 28,153 is the number of sex discrimination claims brought between April 2006 and April 2007.
⇨ £6,724 is the average award for sex discrimination.
⇨ 30,000 is the number of women in the UK leaving their jobs each year due to pregnancy discrimination.

Work-life balance

In the past work-life balance was considered a women's issue. It is now recognised as a business imperative for attracting and retaining highly productive employees of both sexes.

⇨ Four out of five employees state that work-life balance considerations play a crucial role in deciding whether to stay with or leave their current employer.
⇨ 87% is the proportion of executive candidates rejecting a job due to work-life balance considerations.
⇨ 49% of employers have seen an increase in productivity following the implementation of work-life balance options.
⇨ One-quarter of female employees and one-tenth of male employees have some form of flexible working arrangement.

Care

Understanding carers will increasingly become a significant consideration for employers.

⇨ Care is not a gender issue. Seven out of ten carers under 50 and eight out of ten carers aged 50-60 give up work to care.
⇨ Over the next 30 years, the number of carers in the UK will increase from 6 million to 9 million.
⇨ Three out of five is the number of people who will care for someone at some point in their life.
⇨ There are 3 million working carers in the UK. Of these 1.4 million are men and 1.7 million are women.

82.8p is the amount a woman earns for every pound that a man earns

---

Childcare

Considerations of childcare affect mothers and fathers.

⇨ 12.8 million is the number of working age parents with dependent children.
⇨ £152 is the typical cost per week for a nursery place for a child under two.
⇨ £962 is the annual amount saved by each lower-rate tax-paying parent making use of an employer childcare voucher scheme.
⇨ Increasingly, fathers are taking a greater role in caring for children. In the UK, fathers in two-parent families carry out an average of one-quarter of the family's childcare-related activities during the week, and one-third at weekends.
⇨ Women currently spend twice as much time on housework and on childcare as men.

January 2008

⇨ The above information is reprinted with kind permission from Opportunity Now. Visit www.opportunitynow.org.uk for more information.

© Opportunity Now

Women in non-traditional training and employment

Executive summary of a working paper on occupational segregation by the Equal Opportunities Commission

This is a small, though rigorous study and captures the perspectives of women who have succeeded in entering training or employment in the non-traditional sectors of plumbing, construction, engineering and information and communications technology (ICT). They are, therefore, the exception in the context of a highly segregated labour market. These women provide valuable information on occupational segregation and gender from an 'insider' perspective.

The focus group method was used to interview six groups of women, 43 in total, who were:
- Training in mainstream environments;
- Training in women-only environments;
- Employed and self-employed in the construction sector.

In addition, six staff from mainstream and women-only training centres took part in individual interviews.

The research was conducted at venues in London, the South East, Yorkshire and Wales with women aged between 20 and 50 years old.

Key findings

Benefits
- Women experienced considerable benefits from training and work in non-traditional skills sectors, and their passion for the work was a feature of the research.
- Women unanimously stated that their choice of training or employment sector had improved the quality of their life, bringing them job satisfaction, empowering them to take control of their lives, and, for some, lifting them out of poverty.
- The construction industry in particular offers scope for self-employment, that enables

By Angela Dale, Nors Jackson, Nicky Hill

women to combine domestic and caring responsibilities and paid work, with the highest levels of flexibility.
- Some of the women had experienced careers in traditionally female areas and were motivated to move into male-dominated sectors for better pay.

Women in training and employment faced overt and covert discrimination from employers

- There was evidence that employers were recognising the benefits to business of employing more women. Some customers in diverse households are happier to have tradeswomen in their homes. Women needed to be more highly skilled than men to succeed, therefore made highly skilled and committed employees. Women tended to have communication and interpersonal skills that enable businesses to be more competitive and responsive in a changing labour market.

Obstacles
- Although women's experiences differed, there is compelling evidence of the range of obstacles and challenges faced in entering training and employment. In order to succeed in the present climate those women have had to become particularly resilient and determined.
- Many women had been interested in non-traditional occupations

when younger, though had been actively discouraged or unsupported from teachers and careers advisers when at school or in further education.
- Women had not been given appropriate advice and guidance in subject choices for non-traditional route ways, nor when older in relation to training provision.
- Some women encountered resistance to them undertaking non-traditional skills training from their husbands or partners. Success in a male domain, coupled with the fact that they could earn more money than their partner, triggered resentment.
- Women found it much harder than their male counterparts to secure work experience placements with employers in order to complete their NVQ qualifications.
- In mainstream training women experienced isolation as the 'only one' on many courses, with no female lecturers, inflexible hours and little support. These conditions meant that only the strongest and most determined women completed the courses.
- As many of the women entered non-traditional training when older, they had not been eligible to take part in Modern Apprenticeships. Funding to employers for training is focused

upon Modern Apprenticeships, therefore the options for women were limited by age and gender.

⇨ Women in training and employment faced overt and covert discrimination from employers. In some cases employers refused to train or employ women. In other cases women were laughed at, bullied, faced antagonism, were given the worst jobs to do and were expected to make the tea.

⇨ The anti-social and inflexible hours of the industries proved deeply problematic for women with childcare and caring responsibilities.

⇨ Although an issue for everybody, health and safety considerations in the manual industries were perceived as a particular obstacle to increasing numbers of women.

What helps?

⇨ It is clear that women need support and active encouragement from individuals to pursue careers in non-traditional skills areas. One key individual who believed in them could make the difference for women in their decision-making.

⇨ The provision of women-only positive action training was instrumental to the success of many women in non-traditional skill areas. Such provision had inspired many to start training.

⇨ Training with peers in numbers, flexible delivery of training, childcare provision, pre-entry skills and entry to employment provision and explicit support mechanisms were key to women's success.

⇨ Good employers were key to women's successful entry into the sectors either through the provision of work-based placements or in securing employment and were equally open to employing women. Their male employees were praised as good colleagues.

⇨ The diversity of the market and changing households are such that people are beginning to ask for tradeswomen. Some employers were recognising the added value and business that employing women could accrue for them.

⇨ Women suggested that their

communication and inter-personal skills were increasingly recognised by employers as important in enhancing their marketability.

⇨ For some women, the importance of equal opportunities policies was underlined as protection for them in employment in the public sector.

⇨ Some employers in the ICT sector were willing to adopt flexible working practices to meet the needs of women trainees.

Implications

It is clear from the research that those women who have succeeded in non-traditional skill areas are particularly resilient and determined. In the context of a highly segregated labour market and the obstacles that women continue to face, it is unrealistic to expect that numbers will significantly increase unless particular actions are instituted. Nor is it reasonable to expect women to be unusually resilient and determined in order to survive in training or work.

It seems that particular attention and positive action is required to meet the needs of women entering training and employment and a national policy is developed. This could be successfully achieved through collaboration between major organisations and stakeholders like the DFES, QCA, LSC, Sector Skills Councils, Women's Training Network and The UK SET Resource Centre.

Suggestions

The following actions are suggested to re-address the needs of women entering training and employment in non-traditional skills areas:

⇨ Girls are encouraged and supported to undertake work placements and choose vocational options in non-traditional skill areas.

⇨ Girls are introduced to role-models of women working in non-traditional skill areas.

⇨ Careers and connexions advisers are trained to counter gender stereotyping in career choice.

⇨ Positive action training is highlighted and marketed to women.

⇨ Features of positive action training for women are taken into the mainstream and adopted as good practice.

⇨ Positive action training provision is supported and developed in every local labour market.

⇨ New adult apprenticeships are developed for women.

⇨ Employers are encouraged to provide quality work placements to women in training .

⇨ Employers give women a chance in employment so that they can demonstrate what they are capable of.

⇨ Employers develop flexible working practices.

⇨ Employers develop equal opportunities policies and practices (including harassment) to develop their workforce and provide protection to women.

⇨ The above information is reprinted with kind permission from the Equal Opportunities Commission, now part of the Commission for Equality and Human Rights. Visit www.cehr.org.uk for more information.

© Equal Opportunities Commission

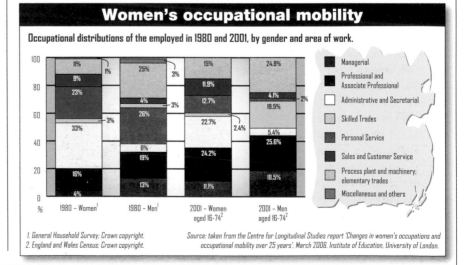

Women's occupational mobility

Occupational distributions of the employed in 1980 and 2001, by gender and area of work.

Legend:
- Managerial
- Professional and Associate Professional
- Administrative and Secretarial
- Skilled Trades
- Personal Service
- Sales and Customer Service
- Process plant and machinery; elementary trades
- Miscellaneous and others

1980 – Women[1]: 11%, 9%, 23%, 33%, 16%, 4%
1980 – Men[1]: 1%, 25%, 26%, 6%, 19%, 13%
2001 – Women aged 16-74[2]: 3%, 15%, 11.9%, 12.7%, 22.7%, 24.2%, 11.1%
2001 – Men aged 16-74[2]: 24.9%, 4.1%, 19.5%, 5.4%, 25.6%, 18.5%, 2%, 2.4%

1. General Household Survey; Crown copyright.
2. England and Wales Census; Crown copyright.

Source: taken from the Centre for Longitudinal Studies report 'Changes in women's occupations and occupational mobility over 25 years', March 2006, Institute of Education, University of London.

Better jobs for women still scarce

Information from the European Association for Education of Adults

Women are continuing to drive employment growth in Europe, but remain disadvantaged on the labour market in relation to men, says a report adopted by the European Commission today. Despite higher educational attainment, women continue to be employed less and paid less than men. The 2008 report on equality between women and men will be transmitted to EU leaders at the Spring Summit on 8-9 March.

'Our strategy for growth and jobs has been successful in creating more jobs for women in the EU,' said Equal Opportunities Commissioner Vladimír Špidla. 'But ongoing challenges like the pay gap, labour market segregation, and work/life balance mean we still have some way to go to make those jobs "better" jobs too. Overall, despite their better educational attainment, women's careers are shorter, slower and less well-paid: it is clear that we need to do more to make full use of the productive potential of the workforce.'

The Commission report highlights that the quantitative progress of women on the labour market has not yet been matched in qualitative terms. On the one hand, more than 7.5 out of the 12 million new jobs created in the EU since 2000 have been taken by women. Their employment rate now stands at 57.2%, or 3.5 points above its 2000 level, compared with a less than one point rise in the rate of male employment over the same period. Similarly, the rise in the rate of employment of women over the age of 55 has been significantly faster than that of men, and now stands at 34.8%, i.e. a 7.4 points increase on 2000.

On the other hand, several aspects of the quality of women's work remain problematic. Despite the fact that women represent 59% of university graduates and have a better educational attainment, their employment rate remains lower than men's (by 14.4 points) and they continue to earn on average 15% less than men for every hour worked.

Women also face greater difficulties in reaching decision-making positions. The presence of female managers in companies is progressing very slowly and stands at only 33%. Work/life balance is one area where major differences persist between women and men. The employment rate of women with young children is only 62.4%, compared with 91.4% for men with children. And women have a disproportionately high recourse to part-time work (32.9%) compared with men (7.7%), underlining the imbalance between men and women in the use of time.

The report underlines that more efforts need to be made to create more and better jobs. The creation of more jobs must go hand in hand with an improvement in quality. Quality jobs attract workers and allow them to fully exploit their productive potential and contribute to improving the quality of life in society as a whole. Equality between women and men is an essential quality component of work, says the report. Special attention should also be given to improving both the supply and quality of services to help people balance professional and private life, in order to allow men and women with dependants to (re-) enter and stay on the labour market.

In addition, getting rid of stereotypes is essential to promoting equality between women and men, as they continue to influence the choice of education, training or employment, participation in domestic and family duties, and representation in decision-making jobs.

24 January 2008

⇨ The above information is re-printed with kind permission from the European Association for Education of Adults. Visit www.eaea.org for more information.

© European Association for Education of Adults

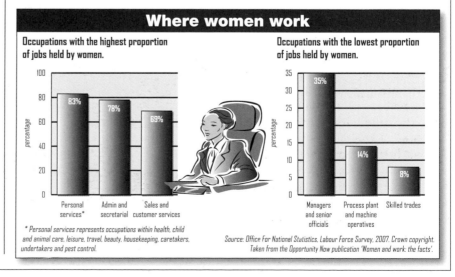

Where women work

Occupations with the highest proportion of jobs held by women.

Personal services*: 83%
Admin and secretarial: 78%
Sales and customer services: 69%

Occupations with the lowest proportion of jobs held by women.

Managers and senior officials: 35%
Process plant and machine operatives: 14%
Skilled trades: 8%

* Personal services represents occupations within health, child and animal care, leisure, travel, beauty, housekeeping, caretakers, undertakers and pest control.

Source: Office For National Statistics, Labour Force Survey, 2007. Crown copyright. Taken from the Opportunity Now publication 'Women and work: the facts'.

Want a difficult job done? Then ask a woman

Information from the Chartered Institute of Personnel and Development

A large number of business leaders will only appoint a woman into a very senior post in times of crisis and poor performance, according to a new report from the Chartered Institute of Personnel and Development (CIPD). This leaves female leaders facing a form of hidden discrimination which leaves them more likely to fail than their male counterparts.

The CIPD commissioned Exeter University to carry out the new research, *Women in the boardroom: the risks of being at the top*, which exposes the hidden problem that employers face in increasing the number of women in senior jobs. Research conducted by the University of Exeter finds:

⇨ women are more readily appointed to tough jobs that are perceived to lead to make-or-break outcomes in terms of career success, than men.

⇨ in crisis situations business leaders are more inclined to open up job opportunities to women, leaving women business leaders at greater risk of failing than their male colleagues working at the same levels.

Dianah Worman, CIPD Diversity Adviser, says: 'Female leaders are all too often set up to fail. Due to limited opportunities open to female leaders many are forced to take the more difficult jobs in organisations with a history of poor performance, perpetuating the myth that women are poor performers in senior positions, and covering up the true extent of discrimination for the most desirable senior management positions.

'But the growth in the number of successful small businesses owned by women goes some way to indicate their business and leadership capabilities and highlights the talent other large organisations are missing. So old-fashioned attitudes are not only unfair and discriminatory towards women but they leave organisations shooting themselves in the foot.

'It is in the best interests of business to take action to enable achievement rather than sitting back and hoping for the best – organisations need to open their doors to the leadership capabilities of both halves of the population, regardless of the performance of the organisation.

'Being prepared in this way will give employers access to a larger pool of talent and enable them to select the best person for the job regardless of sex and go some way to help organisations to avoid crisis situations or navigate them better when they do.'

The report pulls research together that shows women are more likely to be appointed at a time when organisations experience poor performance and often set up to fail:

⇨ Company performance leading up to the appointment of a director differs depending on the gender of the appointee: for FTSE 100 companies that appointed men to their boards of directors, share price performance was relatively stable, both before and after the appointment. However, in a time of a general financial downturn in the stock market, companies that appointed a woman had experienced consistently poor performance in the months preceding the appointment (Ryan and Haslam 2005).

⇨ Business leaders are more likely to select the female candidate when the company's performance was said to be declining than when it was improving: a study of 83 senior managers participating in a regional Business Leaders' Forum (Haslam and Ryan 2006, Study 4). In a scenario that involved appointing a financial director to a company these business leaders were much more likely to see the female candidate as suitable for the position when the organisation was experiencing a marked downturn in performance.

⇨ Research findings also support the notion that the glass cliff can be seen as an opportunity (Haslam and Ryan 2006): in response to a scenario involving the appointment of a financial director, business leaders believed that a risky situation was seen to provide a male candidate with a much lower quality of opportunity than a non-risky situation. However, the opposite was true for an equally qualified female candidate.

19 March 2007

⇨ The above information is reprinted with kind permission from the Chartered Institute of Personnel and Development. Visit www.cipd.co.uk for more information.

© CIPD

UK gender pay gap worst in Europe

Information from iVillage UK

According to the government's Women and Work Commission, in the 30 years since pay discrimination was outlawed, women are still earning 17 per cent less than men, a figure which could potentially cost the UK economy £23 billion a year. In response to the commission's findings, the government has released new policies to tackle gender inequalities in pay, but will they be enough?

By Peggy Nuttall and Clare Spurrell

According to the Fawcett Society, under the current system it will be 80 years before women working full-time earn as much as their male counterparts, and 140 years before part-time female workers catch up with men. Despite girls consistently outperforming boys at GCSE, A-level and degree, findings show that within three years of graduating women are earning less than men. In the UK, over half of all women are currently working jobs *beneath* their skills and qualifications.

Inequality starts in the classroom

According to the Equal Opportunities Commission (EOC) 15 per cent of young people in school are neither given advice nor encouraged into work experience placements in professions dominated by the opposite sex – with women often opting for badly paid careers such as nursing or teaching over science or engineering.

The government's response in schools is being praised by most, and involves introducing new schemes to give young girls better understanding of the wider choice of careers available to them, and encouraging them to consider work experience placements in more non-traditional roles.

Is the government missing the point?

More worrying is that female school leavers choosing 'women specific roles' – such as the caring professions

– are being paid 17 per cent less than men in more traditional 'masculine roles' such as driving and building, despite both requiring the same level of skill.

The Commission's response to this seems to miss the point. Instead of closing the gap between wages of men and women in careers that require similar skill levels, the government is instead planning to spend £20 million to raise the skill level of women working in these roles, encouraging them to change careers altogether. This policy will only reduce the available 'woman-power' in these

lower paid jobs. 'You can't simply try and persuade all childcare workers to become lorry drivers,' says Jenny Westaway of the Fawcett Society. 'What we have to do is revalue the kind of work that women are doing such as cleaning, catering and caring for others – we've got to value it more highly.'

'We are disappointed that Women and Work didn't back a compulsory pay audit,' says Westaway. 'This would require employers to look at what they're paying women and men, look at the kind of jobs and judge whether they are of equal value, making sure they are not discriminating either inadvertently or consciously.'

Children cost mothers more than fathers

Although women are less likely to ask for more money at work than men, a bigger factor to work inequality is children. According to the London School of Economics, mothers who returned to their previous jobs as part-timers quickly fell behind their male colleagues financially, and those

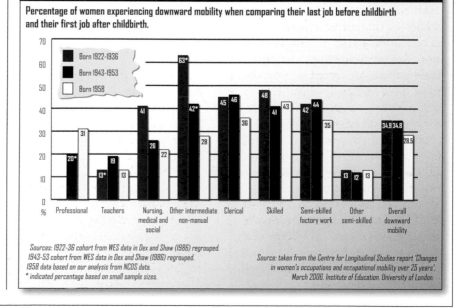

Downward mobility for new mothers

Percentage of women experiencing downward mobility when comparing their last job before childbirth and their first job after childbirth.

Legend: Born 1922-1936; Born 1943-1953; Born 1958

Categories (Professional, Teachers, Nursing medical and social, Other intermediate non-manual, Clerical, Skilled, Semi-skilled factory work, Other semi-skilled, Overall downward mobility):

Professional: 20*, 31
Teachers: 13*, 19, 13
Nursing, medical and social: 41, 26, 22
Other intermediate non-manual: 63*, 42*, 28
Clerical: 45, 46, 36
Skilled: 48, 41, 43
Semi-skilled factory work: 42, 44, 35
Other semi-skilled: 13, 12, 13
Overall downward mobility: 34.9, 34.8, 28.5

Sources: 1922-36 cohort from WES data in Dex and Shaw (1986) regrouped. 1943-53 cohort from WES data in Dex and Shaw (1986) regrouped. 1958 data based on our analysis from NCDS data.
* indicated percentage based on small sample sizes.

Source: taken from the Centre for Longitudinal Studies report 'Changes in women's occupations and occupational mobility over 25 years'. March 2006. Institute of Education, University of London.

that entered new jobs on a part-time basis did even worse.

According to the recent findings by the government's Women and Work Commission, full-time working women currently earn 17 per cent less than men, but for part-time women this falls to 38 per cent, meaning that a part-time woman earns a mere 59 pence for every pound earned by her male counterpart. Considering that in 1975, when the Equal Pay Act came in, the part-time pay gap was 40 per cent, it's strikingly obvious that it isn't closing.

Currently, many companies still conform to 'stuffed shirt' policies that have no openings for part-time workers in senior positions. This is forcing a large workforce of highly skilled and qualified women with young children out of the boardroom, because they cannot deliver a 40-plus-hour week, and into jobs below their capabilities.

Multi-million-pound plans are promised in the upcoming budget to provide women returning to work after having a child greater support, but many believe change must come from within. 'We want employers to be more imaginative about the range of jobs that can be done part-time' Westaway explains. 'It might take some effort to get used to a new way of working, but there's evidence to show that this kind of working will increase retention and recruitment rates – it will pay dividends in the end.'

The Women and Work Commission, headed by Margaret Prosser, plans to change these attitudes at senior management level, by introducing a pilot project aimed at blue-chip companies to offer part-time senior management positions to women. They hope that this will prove flexibility at senior level will not lead to a loss of profit or productivity.

What can we do?

One American academic, Linda Hirshman, believes that women should take the matter into their own hands, offering a radical solution to ensure career success and achieve the 'have-it-all' lifestyle. She insists that women should shun creative, philosophical or arts-based degrees at university, and favour studying law and medicine – specifically plastic surgery!

Hirshman advises women to marry a man who is 'beneath' them (an artist ideally) and only have one child – if you must have any at all. This formula, says Hirshman, centres on the notion that the partner with the weaker profession (and salary) is more likely to sacrifice their career for the family, thus ensuring women bag a stay-at-home dad. Plus, one child is more manageable financially, professionally and emotionally, any more (according to Hirshman) is career suicide.

Fawcett are not convinced. 'We'd say Hirshman's solution is not our solution! But I think we're thinking of a common problem,' admits Westaway. 'First we've got to close the pay gap so there aren't different earnings within a partnership. We've got to encourage men to take on more caring roles and engage more with the work/life balance – allowing a more level playing field between the sexes at work'.

A more realistic solution may be to follow the employment practices of some of our European neighbours. By adopting practices such as requesting all employers with 10 or more employees to provide gender-divided wage statistics, develop equality plans, corrective measures and annual pay revisions, countries like Denmark and Sweden are way ahead of the game when it comes to the gender pay gap. Despite having the same levels of female employment as the UK, their pay gaps are far lower, and still reducing.

⇨ The above information is re-printed with kind permission from iVillage UK. Visit www.iVillage.co.uk for more information.

© iVillage UK

Being positive

If we think sexual equality is a good principle, should we be more active in enabling women to advance?

Inequality between the sexes has a long history and has been tackled in earnest only in the last few decades. Many people would say that although progress has been made, for example with equal pay and sexual discrimination legislation, there is still much to be done. Should we be more active about this and practise positive discrimination?

Positive discrimination (or a close relative, affirmative action) means that active steps are taken to advance minority groups, with preference given to someone on the basis of an attribute, such as sex, that would previously have caused them to be discriminated against.

While the motivations may be honourable, positive discrimination can easily be seen as a form of double standards – where some individuals or groups do not need to achieve the standards required of others. This can lead to resentment and to devaluation of the people selected, who may be perceived as 'substandard'.

The emphasis today therefore tends to be on removing barriers to participation, so there is equality of opportunity. This may take many forms, such as promotion of opportunities among particular groups – campaigns to encourage women to think about a career in engineering, for example.

It can be seen as a way of removing barriers that have inhibited these groups from advancing in the past, perhaps due to prejudice or lack of opportunity.

More generally, there is a greater focus on individuals and their qualities or potential, rather than their academic qualifications or other achievements.

⇨ The above information is reprinted with kind permission from the Wellcome Trust, a charity funding research to improve human and animal health. Visit www.wellcome.ac.uk for more information.

© Wellcome Trust

Gender pay gap

Narrowest since records began

The gender pay gap (as measured by the median hourly pay excluding overtime of full-time employees) narrowed between 2006 and 2007 to its lowest value since records began. The gap between women's median hourly pay and men's was 12.6 per cent, compared with a gap of 12.8 per cent recorded in April 2006. The median hourly rate for men went up 2.8 per cent to £11.96, while the rate for women increased by 3.1 per cent to £10.46.

The gender pay gap narrowed between 2006 and 2007 to its lowest value since records began

The largest difference was in the South East region, where women's median pay was 15.9 per cent less than men's. The smallest gap was in Northern Ireland, at 2.8 per cent.

On the internationally comparable measure based on mean earnings, women's average hourly pay (excluding overtime) was 17.2 per cent less than men's pay, showing a decrease on the comparable figure of 17.5 per cent for 2006.

In 2007, median weekly earnings of full-time employees for women of £394 were 21 per cent less than those for men (£498), unchanged from 2006.

Women's weekly earnings, including overtime, were lower than men's. This was partly because they worked fewer paid hours per week. Based on hourly earnings excluding overtime, women's earnings increased more slowly across the bottom 10 per cent of the distribution than men's, with a growth of 3.0 per cent compared with 3.7 per cent for their male counterparts. The hourly earnings of the top 10 per cent grew by 2.8 per cent and 3.2 per cent respectively.

Although median hourly pay provides a useful comparison between the earnings of men and women, it does not necessarily indicate differences in rates of pay for comparable jobs. Pay medians are affected by the different work patterns of men and women, such as the proportions in different occupations and their length of time in jobs.

Source: Annual Survey of Hours and Earnings (ASHE)

On the internationally comparable measure based on mean earnings, women's average hourly pay (excluding overtime) was 17.2 per cent less than men's pay

Notes

⇨ The median is the value below which 50 per cent of employees fall.

⇨ Pay refers to gross pay (before tax) of full-time employees on adult rates whose pay for the survey week was unaffected by absence.

⇨ The Annual Survey of Hours and Earnings is based on a sample of employee jobs taken from HM Revenue & Customs records. The 2007 ASHE is based on approximately 142,000 returns. In 2007 information was collected for the pay period that included 18 April.

7 November 2007

⇨ The above information is re-printed with kind permission from the Office for National Statistics. Visit www.statistics.gov.uk for more information.

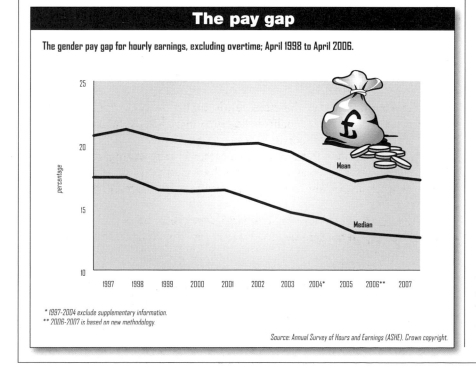

The pay gap

The gender pay gap for hourly earnings, excluding overtime; April 1998 to April 2006.

percentage

25

20

15

10

Mean

Median

1997   1998   1999   2000   2001   2002   2003   2004*   2005   2006**   2007

* 1997-2004 exclude supplementary information.
** 2006-2007 is based on new methodology.

Source: Annual Survey of Hours and Earnings (ASHE). Crown copyright.

Pay gap 'costs women £300,000 over lifetime'

By Laura Clout

Professional women are still blocked by a 'glass ceiling' which sees them earn almost 27 per cent less than their male counterparts, official figures show.

The data suggest women's progress at senior management level continues to be hampered by the demands of balancing work with bringing up a family.

Where a man would earn an annual wage of £70,657, a woman with a similar position would earn £56,933.

The gender pay gap narrowed by just 0.3 per cent over the past year and campaign groups say that at the current rate of progress, it will take an estimated 20 years to close.

A lack of well-paid part-time jobs, limited pension provision and shorter working lives mean that, compared with men, women are almost always short-changed.

Figures from the Office of National Statistics (ONS) reveal the overall gender pay gap between full-time employees is 17.2 per cent.

The divide is most marked in senior management – where women earn 26.8 per cent less per hour than their male equivalents. This equates to a salary of £48,651 for a male director, compared with just £35,588 for a woman in the same position.

Baroness Prosser, deputy chairman of the Equality and Human Rights Commission, said: 'Women who work full-time are cheated of around £330,000 over the course of their lifetime. This is not just about an extra pair of shoes for a night out.

'Nationwide, women are less able to save for a pension, leaving them poverty-stricken in old age. The low wages of many single mums leaves them struggling.'

When the Equal Pay Act was implemented more than 30 years ago, women received an average of 37 per cent less pay than men. Campaigners say efforts to close the gap have stalled.

The ONS figures also show that jobs held by women were far more likely to pay below the minimum wage.

A separate study by the Institute of Directors showed that the gap in the boardroom widened over the past year from 19 per cent to 22 per cent. The institute said its survey of almost 4,000 directors showed the biggest gaps were in the service and voluntary sectors, where women's salaries were as much as 26 per cent lower.

8 November 2007

Waiting for equal pay

It is appalling that it may take 80 years to achieve equal pay. There is no point waiting for tribunals to narrow the gap. The state must force change through the statute book

By Madeleine Bunting

The pay gap between men and women is one of those issues that generates a peculiar amount of wishful thinking, breezy assumptions and ignorance. Companies insist they don't have a problem, women don't know if they have a problem, and men just keep mum. The size of our pay packet is one of the last parts of our lives to remain private – and it's in too many people's interests to keep it that way. So any blast of publicity is welcome on this everyday outrage, and the figures published yesterday usefully explode some myths about the gender pay gap.

They trashed one of the oldest comforts trotted out at regular intervals over the 32 years since the Equal Pay Act came into force, namely that the gap would simply disappear of its own sweet accord as more women moved up the career ladder. But the Chartered Management Institute's survey showed that although women are proving exceptionally talented and getting promotion well ahead of their male counterparts, these achievements have had no impact on closing the pay gap. Rather than shrinking, the gap has widened slightly, to 12.2%.

But that figure masks how truly dire some sectors are: take the food and drink industry, for instance, where male managers earned 46% more than their female counterparts; or look at sectors such as human resources, pensions and insurance, all of which clocked up gaps of more than 40%. These companies should be named and shamed. How are the supermarkets where you shop, and the insurance companies which hold your policies, allowed to get away with this? Forget all the excuses and good intentions churned out by these big companies over the years, or the fancy equal opportunities initiatives they've signed up to – if they wanted to sort out the pay gap, they could do so. The fact that the pay gap in the public sector is now a minuscule 0.7% demonstrates that it can be done.

The pay gap between men and women is one of those issues that generates a peculiar amount of wishful thinking, breezy assumptions and ignorance

---

Put these figures to an old hand like Professor Linda Gratton of the Lehman Centre at the London Business School, who published a major study of women in business earlier this year, and she is horrified: 'This is outrageous. Why aren't more women taking their employers to court? Women are getting a really bad deal, yet we know from the research that they are just as high performers as men.'

But women are going to court. There has been a 155% increase in equal pay cases just over the last year,

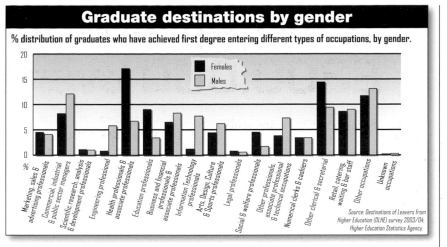

Graduate destinations by gender

% distribution of graduates who have achieved first degree entering different types of occupations, by gender.

Source: Destinations of Leavers from Higher Education (DLHE) survey 2003/04, Higher Education Statistics Agency.

and the tribunal system is collapsing under the strain. The point is that the Equal Pay Act is well past its sell-by date. It puts the onus on individual women to challenge injustice – it's rather like telling a homeowner to sue his burglar himself. Thousands of cases have to be heard individually, clogging the process; thousands more women are deterred, unwilling to rock the boat. There are more effective ways to bring about change than on a case-by-case basis through tribunals. Small legislative changes could make a big difference. At the moment, companies are terrified of pay reviews for fear of litigation if they reveal discrimination. If they had a two-year transition period to put things right, they might be more willing to do the review.

The government has been inexcusably lazy. Progress seems to have stalled. Since Labour came to power in 1997 the pay gap has closed by less than 3%; progress since the Equal Pay Act in 1975 has been painfully slow, falling from 29% to just over 17%. It could be another 80 years before we achieve pay parity – my putative

granddaughter might be a beneficiary if she's lucky, but not my daughter.

Labour has done precious little apart from bringing in the minimum wage, which boosted the earnings of the low paid, of whom a disproportionate number are women. But that was about combating poverty rather than achieving equality – the latter remains a Cinderella of Labour history. Ruth Kelly, when in charge of the equality brief, sat on her hands.

The most insidious aspect of the issue has been the 'blame the victim' game. As government washes its hands and private sector companies mouth platitudes, women get the blame. It's reported that they don't ask for pay rises, they don't negotiate, they don't care about the money as much as men. But new research in the US shows that all these study findings are true for a good reason: women who are seen to be pushy and demanding are disproportionately penalised – while such behaviour in men is rewarded. The odds are stacked against women. In no other area of national life do we expect the victims to deliver justice for themselves, so why on the pay gap?

With Kelly gone and Harriet Harman promising mandatory pay reviews (that will prove a merry fight with No 10) in her deputy leadership campaign, and Barbara Follett as the junior equality minister, there's a new mood of optimism that the government might finally put its shoulder to the wheel. Findings like those published yesterday might even manage to stir up the sense of outrage which has been so strangely absent from this 32-year-old saga.

6 September 2007
© *Guardian Newspapers Limited 2008*

PAY GAP

KEY FACTS

⇨ By about 18 months, most children begin to display gender-specific behaviours. Boys will tend to choose vehicles or construction toys to play with; girls go for dolls. These behaviours appear so early that some suggest that they must be innate, while others argue that they simply reflect parental influences or the child's desire to conform. (page 1)

⇨ Increasingly 'breadwinner dads' and 'stay at home mums' are a thing of the past. (page 2)

⇨ Women earn on average 17% per hour less than men for full-time work. (page 5)

⇨ Sex equality will take generations to achieve at the current 'painfully slow' rate of progress, the Equal Opportunities Commission (EOC) said. (page 6)

⇨ Only 2 out of 17 (12%) editors of national newspapers are women, while all but one of the 17 deputy editors surveyed are men. (page 11)

⇨ The majority of the world's poor are women: around 70 per cent of the 1.3 billion people who live in extreme poverty, on less than one dollar a day, are women and girls. (page 12)

⇨ In the majority of the world, women are still seen as second-class citizens, and young women and girls particularly so; the property of their fathers until they are married and of their husbands after they have tied the knot. The more patriarchal a society, the more sons are preferred. (page 13)

⇨ Men have a less traditional view of gender roles than they did 20 years ago. Yet according to the latest British Social Attitudes report, women are still far more likely than men to do the household chores. (page 15)

⇨ Almost a third of men of all ages (30%) say it is important to have their home look the way they want it to, rising to almost four in ten (37%) amongst 30- to 34-year-olds. (page 16)

⇨ Academics have found a high level of gender segregation in people's working lifestyles, with women generally earning less and struggling to break into senior management roles. (page 17)

⇨ 29% of EU27 women are employed part-time compared with 7% of men. (page 18)

⇨ Women's political values are more pro-equality and they are looking to Government to do more to promote women's chances. (page 21)

⇨ Converging evidence from a variety of sources (historical exam records for England, Foundation Stage and Key Stage results, international evidence and current results) shows that the gender gap is wide in English and narrower in Maths, with, on average, girls performing better than boys. The gender gap in the Sciences has been traditionally very small. (page 22)

⇨ Girls are more likely to stay on in full-time education at age 16 (82 per cent of girls and 72 per cent of boys). Girls are also more likely to be entered for A-levels than boys (54 per cent of entries are female), in contrast to the 1950s and 1960s when only a third of A-level entries were female. (page 22)

⇨ It has been hypothesised that the gender mix of teachers could play a role in the observed gender gap in attainment but this is difficult to measure and there is no strong evidence to date that this is the case. (page 25)

⇨ While girls are now achieving better academic results than boys at age 16, relatively few young women are choosing science or science-related subjects for further study. (page 26)

⇨ A study of people now in their 40s has revealed that those who went to single-sex schools were more likely to study subjects not traditionally associated with their gender than those who went to co-educational schools. Girls from single-sex schools also went on to earn more than those from co-educational schools. (page 27)

⇨ In choosing future careers nearly six in ten girls (57%) received information about going into teaching and over two-fifths (43%) about working in childcare. Conversely less than a third were told about the opportunities to work in IT (29%) or business and entrepreneurship (28%), only a fifth were informed about engineering (21%) and fewer than one in ten received enough information about construction (9%) or plumbing (6%). (page 28)

⇨ Increasing women's participation in the labour market and reducing gender segregation in the workplace is estimated to be worth between £15 billion and £23 billion to the UK economy. (page 29)

⇨ Despite the fact that women represent 59% of university graduates in Europe and have a better educational attainment, their employment rate remains lower than men's (by 14.4 points) and they continue to earn on average 15% less than men for every hour worked. (page 33)

⇨ Women account for only 35% of managers and senior officials. (page 33)

Gender

Gender is based on traits or characteristics that may be either masculine (strength, courage) or feminine (nurturing, caring) and encompasses both what people imagine themselves to be and the social context in which they find themselves. This is distinct from sex which refers to an individual's biology, but the two terms may sometimes mistakenly be used interchangeably.

Gender Equality Duty

The new Gender Equality Duty came into force in April 2007. It means all public bodies, including hospitals, local authorities, schools and the police must take gender into consideration when providing services.

Gender roles

The term 'gender roles' tends to refer to the tasks and activities traditionally done by either men or women. For example, in the past a woman was expected to be responsible for housework and childcare, while a man would be the 'breadwinner' and earn money for the family. As society has moved further towards equality, many people have rejected the idea that men and women should have specific roles within society based on their gender, but statistics show that women are still more likely to take responsibility for childcare and household chores.

Gender stereotypes

As with other groups, people of specific genders are susceptible to stereotyping. Women may be presumed to have a more nurturing nature than men, to obsess over their appearance, or to enjoy certain types of books and films ('chick flicks'), among other things. Similarly, men may be supposed to enjoy sports, drink excessively and find it harder than women to express emotions. However, as with any stereotype these are generalisations not true of everyone, and can be offensive if they are assumed based only on someone's gender. If a stereotype is taken to the extreme, this can also be seen as discrimination (for example, if a female employee is always expected to make the tea because this is 'a woman's job').

Glass ceiling

The term 'glass ceiling' refers to the problem of professional advancement sometimes faced by women at work. They are prevented from advancing upwards, in spite of holding relevant qualifications, due to sex discrimination or other factors related to their gender. However, as this barrier is not official it may not be obvious to others.

Glass cliff

The so-called 'glass cliff' phenomenon might be called the opposite of the glass ceiling. In a glass cliff situation, a woman will be promoted to a position of importance in which she has been set up to fail.

Pay gap

The pay gap refers to the difference between men and women's earnings. Currently, women earn on average 17% less than their male counterparts.

Positive discrimination

Sometimes called affirmative action, this means that active steps are taken to advance minority groups, with preference given to someone on the basis of an attribute, such as sex, that would previously have caused them to be discriminated against. While some people think this practice is necessary to counter the effects of discrimination against women, others feel that it is unfair to choose candidates based partly or entirely on their gender rather than simply the one who is best for the job. Some feel that this practice would cause resentment rather than furthering the cause of equality.

Sex

Sex is a biological concept based on, for example, the possession of particular types of sex cells and organs. Usually (but not always) two sexes can be identified in animals: males and females. Sex is biological, and distinct from the social concept of gender. However, confusion exists over the two terms and they may sometimes be used interchangeably.

Sex discrimination

Treating someone differently because they are male, female or transgendered, resulting in a disadvantage to them in a certain area of life, e.g. employment, education.

INDEX

Additional Resources

Other Issues titles

If you are interested in researching further some of the issues raised in *The Gender Gap*, you may like to read the following titles in the **Issues** series:

⇨ Vol. 155 *Domestic Abuse* (ISBN 978 1 86168 442 4)

⇨ Vol. 139 *The Education Problem* (ISBN 978 1 86168 391 5)

⇨ Vol. 133 *Teen Pregnancy and Lone Parents* (ISBN 978 1 86168 379 3)

⇨ Vol. 126 *The Abortion Debate* (ISBN 978 1 86168 365 6)

⇨ Vol. 124 *Parenting Issues* (ISBN 978 1 86168 363 2)

⇨ Vol. 117 *Self-Esteem and Body Image* (ISBN 978 1 86168 350 2)

⇨ Vol. 107 *Work Issues* (ISBN 978 1 86168 327 4)

⇨ Vol. 106 *Trends in Marriage* (ISBN 978 1 86168 326 7)

⇨ Vol. 105 *Ageing Issues* (ISBN 978 1 86168 325 0)

For more information about these titles, visit our website at www.independence.co.uk/publicationslist

Useful organisations

You may find the websites of the following organisations useful for further research:

⇨ **Commission for Equality and Human Rights:** www.equalityhumanrights.com

⇨ **The Department for Children, Schools and Families:** www.dcsf.gov.uk

⇨ **The Fawcett Society:** www.fawcettsociety.org.uk

⇨ **The F Word:** www.thefword.org.uk

⇨ **The Guide Association:** www.girlguiding.org.uk

⇨ **iVillage UK:** www.iVillage.co.uk

⇨ **NatCen:** www.natcen.ac.uk

⇨ **New Internationalist:** www.newint.org

⇨ **Opportunity Now:** www.opportunitynow.org.uk

⇨ **Oxfam:** www.oxfam.org.uk

⇨ **The Wellcome Trust:** www.wellcome.ac.uk

⇨ **YWCA:** www.ywca.org.uk

ACKNOWLEDGEMENTS

The publisher is grateful for permission to reproduce the following material.

While every care has been taken to trace and acknowledge copyright, the publisher tenders its apology for any accidental infringement or where copyright has proved untraceable. The publisher would be pleased to come to a suitable arrangement in any such case with the rightful owner.

Chapter One: Gender in Society

Upbringing versus biology, © Wellcome Trust, *The gender gap*, © Wellcome Trust, *The gender agenda*, © Equal Opportunities Commission, *Equality for girls*, © YWCA, *Changes since the 1970s*, © Equal Opportunities Commission, *Prevalence of sex discrimination*, © Guardian Newspapers Ltd, *Why men should care about gender stereotypes*, © Alex Gibson, *Do men speak Martian?*, © Telegraph Group Ltd, *Today's girls prefer to look sexy rather than be clever*, © Guardian Newspapers Ltd, *Man made news?*, © Fawcett Society, *International gender equality*, © Oxfam, *Because I am a girl...*, © New Internationalist.

Chapter Two: Equality at Home

Who does the housework?, © NatCen, *Men's changing lifestyles*, © Mintel, *Britain and EU failing to mind the gender gap*, © University of Cambridge, *A bride by any other name*, © Eleanor Turner, *Equality is the way to a woman's heart*, © Fawcett Society.

Chapter Three: Education and Careers

Gender and education, © Crown copyright is reproduced with the permission of Her Majesty's Stationery Office, *Gender and subject choice*, © Crown copyright is reproduced with the permission of Her Majesty's Stationery Office, *Boys and single-sex teaching*, © Associated Newspapers Ltd, *The myth of single-sex schooling*, © Centre for Longitudinal Studies, *Gender bias still blights school careers advice*, © The Guide Association, *Women and work: the facts*, © Opportunity Now, *Women in non-traditional training and employment*, © Equal Opportunities Commission, *Better jobs for women still scarce*, © European Association for Education of Adults, *Want a difficult job done? Then ask a woman*, © Chartered Institute of Personnel and Development, *UK gender pay gap worst in Europe*, © iVillage UK, *Being positive*, © Wellcome Trust, *Gender pay gap*, © Crown copyright is reproduced with the permission of Her Majesty's Stationery Office, *Pay gap 'costs women £300,000 over lifetime'*, © Telegraph Group Ltd, *Waiting for equal pay*, © Guardian Newspapers Ltd.

Photographs

Richard Owen: page 31.
Samantha Woolf: pages 7, 21.
Stock Xchng: pages 9 (Rodolfo Clix), 29 (pat), 38 (svilen001).

Illustrations

Pages 5, 12, 19: Simon Kneebone; pages 14, 34: Bev Aisbett; pages 15, 18, 39: Don Hatcher; pages 17, 20, 22: Angelo Madrid.

Additional editorial by Claire Owen, on behalf of Independence Educational Publishers.

And with thanks to the team: Mary Chapman, Sandra Dennis, Claire Owen and Jan Sunderland.

Lisa Firth
Cambridge
April, 2008